Essential Preparation for

UMAT

UNDERGRADUATE MEDICINE & HEALTH SCIENCES ADMISSION TEST

Series Three

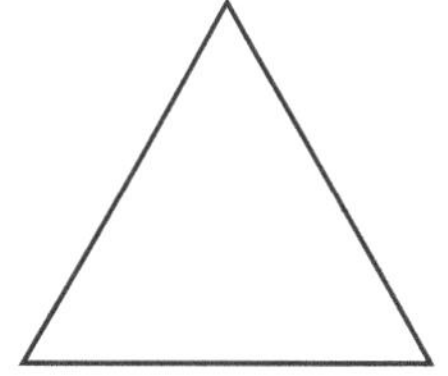

BOOK 3
NON-VERBAL REASONING

Mohan Dhall

Five Senses Education Pty Ltd
2/195 Prospect Highway
Seven Hills 2147
New South Wales
Australia

First Published 2015

Dhall, Mohan
Series 3, Book 3 - Non-Verbal Reasoning

ISBN 978-1-76032-008-9

CONTENTS

Introduction to UMAT Testing Page 4

Non-Verbal Reasoning Questions Page 7

Answers Page 35

Multiple Choice Answer Sheets Page 53

Introduction to UMAT and the Trial Test Papers

Students can gain access into medical training in Australia in one of three ways:

- Through post-graduate entry following the completion of an undergraduate degree. This degree should be in science or science related subjects and the student will need to achieve a high Grade Point Average (GPA).

- Through direct entry based on Year 12 results

- Through performance on the UMAT test and interview (done by each participating university, depending on UMAT results)

The purpose of the UMAT entry test is to assist in the selection of candidates who display the requisite thinking skills and abilities for successful medical training. The test is a 3-hour test completed under exam conditions. There are 134 questions based around three different types of thinking and reasoning:

1. Logical reasoning and problem-solving (48 questions)
2. Understanding people skills (44 questions)
3. Non-verbal reasoning (42 questions)

The follow-up interview performed by participating universities can be quite demanding and can take up to an hour, before a panel of up to three interviewers. Thus preparation and the development of appropriate interview skills and techniques should be practiced, in addition to undertaking test-training.

UMAT Non-Verbal Reasoning Questions

There are 42 practice questions here

Students should aim to take about 55 minutes to complete them. There are practice answer sheets at the end of this book. Try not to mark the pages as you will be able to repeat the questions and test yourself several times.

Instructions to Candidates

The questions here help students to develop and hone their non-verbal thinking skills, and reasoning abilities. There are three different forms of questions presented here:

1. 14 questions where the candidate is to select the alternative that most logically and simply continues the series presented
2. 14 questions where the candidate is to select the alternative that most logically and simply complete the picture
3. 14 questions where the candidate mentally rearranges the five figures to place them in a logical sequence. They are then to select from that sequence the figure that is most logically and simply in the middle.

Questions consist of a sequence or a pattern comprising a number of 'frames' composed of a number of elements. The questions require the identification of the rules that determine the patterns and relationships between the elements from frame to frame, and the application of these rules to find the option (out of a choice of five) that most simply and logically functions as the answer. This requires the generation of appropriate hypotheses and evaluation of evidence to test these hypotheses. Note that different elements may be related by different rules, and different aspects of an element (e.g. orientation and colour) may be governed by different rules. Rules involved in all three types of questions may include:

- movement of elements that is either consistent (same amount each time) or progressive (by increasing amounts);
- changes in size, shape or pattern of elements (consistent or progressive);
- arithmetic relationships;
- combination or disassociation of elements; e.g. 'black + white = white'; 'like elements cancel when superimposed';
- rotation (clockwise or anticlockwise) of elements (consistent or progressive);
- reflection of elements; and symmetry.

Some general hints for arriving at a solution

- Identify the separate elements that make up the sequence or overall pattern.
- Examine each element individually and observe how it is changing. For example:
    - Is the element present in all frames, or does it disappear?
    - Does the number and/or size of the element increase/decrease?
    - Does the position and/or orientation of the element change?
    - Are there changes in shading/pattern?
- Formulate rules for different elements and check that they 'work' for the whole sequence. Rules should be as 'simple' as possible, e.g. smallest increments in rotation or position; shortest sequence of pattern changes; addition before multiplication.
- For each element, use the rule to extend the pattern to determine how it will appear in the answer frame.
- Note also:
    - Determining rules for some elements may help eliminate some options as an answer.
    - It may not always be necessary to determine rules for all elements to arrive at an answer.
    - Sometimes, a definitive answer may only be arrived at by analysing the answer options.

Non-Verbal Reasoning Questions

Question 1

What comes next in this series?

AGD DLV EHF GMW

A) HIJ
B) IJH
C) OLK
D) KNJ
E) LKN

Question 2

Select the alternative that most logically and simply continues the series.

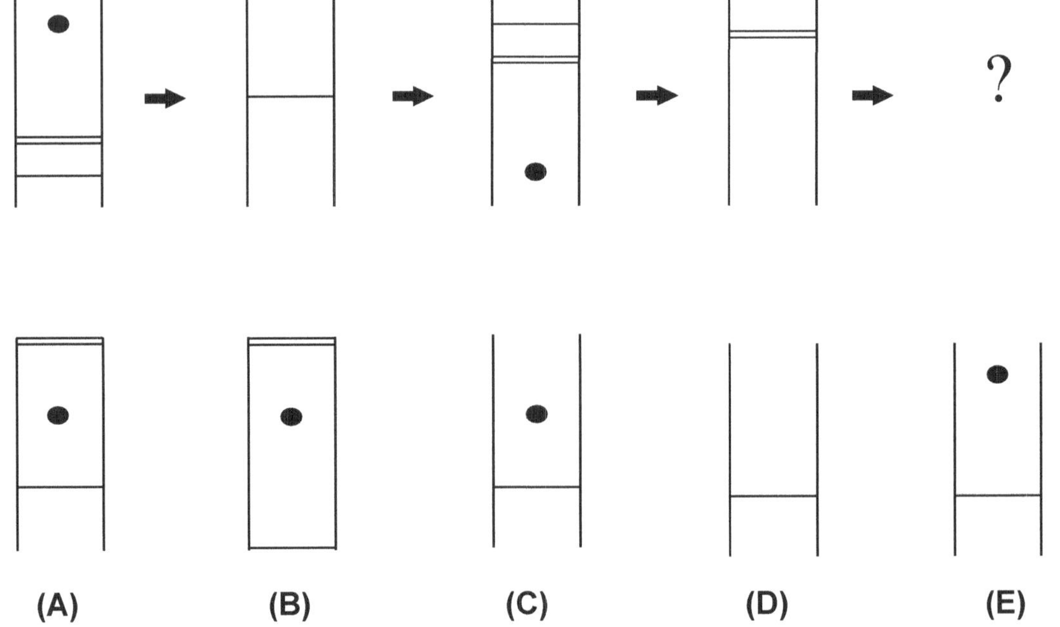

Question 3

Select the alternative that most logically and simply continues the series.

A - F - H - I - ?

Y	W	N	K	Z
(A)	(B)	(C)	(D)	(E)

Question 4

Select the alternative that most logically and simply continues the series.

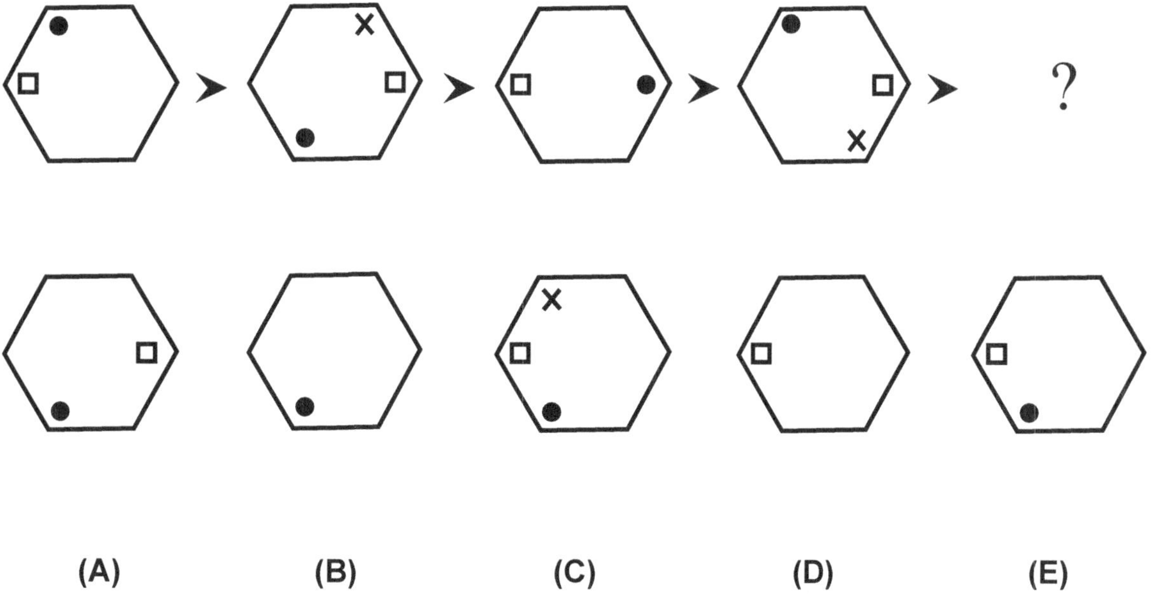

(A) (B) (C) (D) (E)

Question 5

Select the alternative that most logically and simply continues the series.

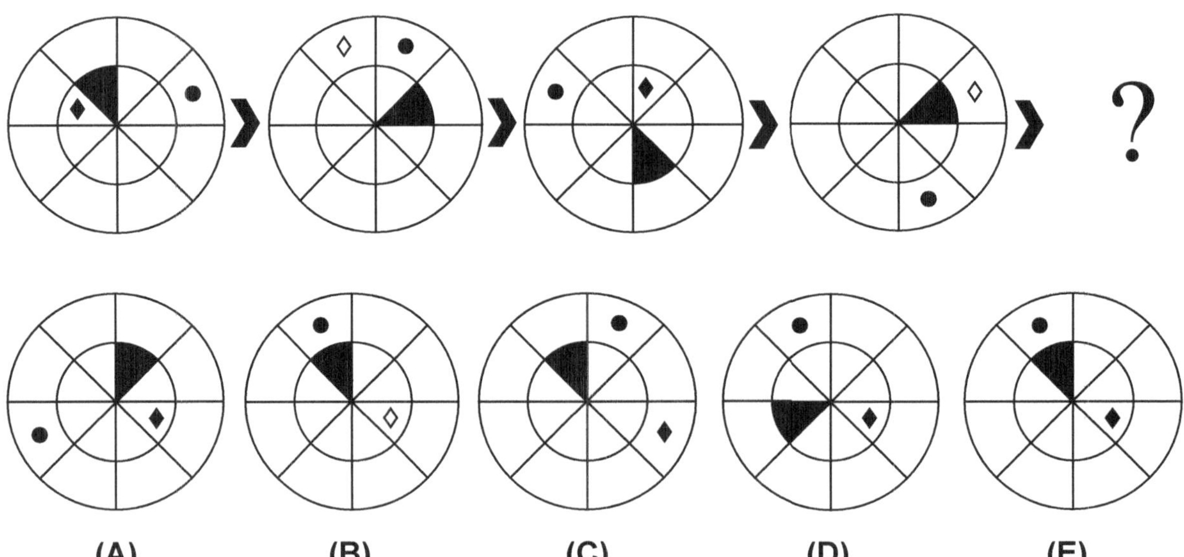

Question 6

Select the alternative that most logically and simply continues the series.

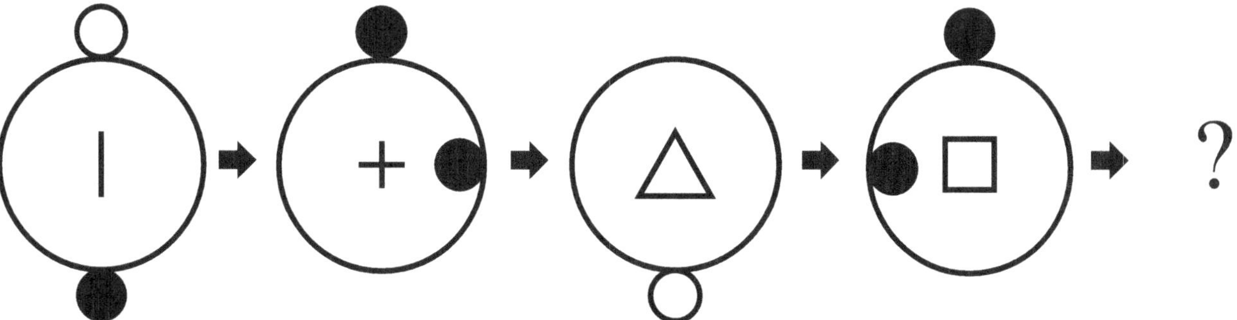

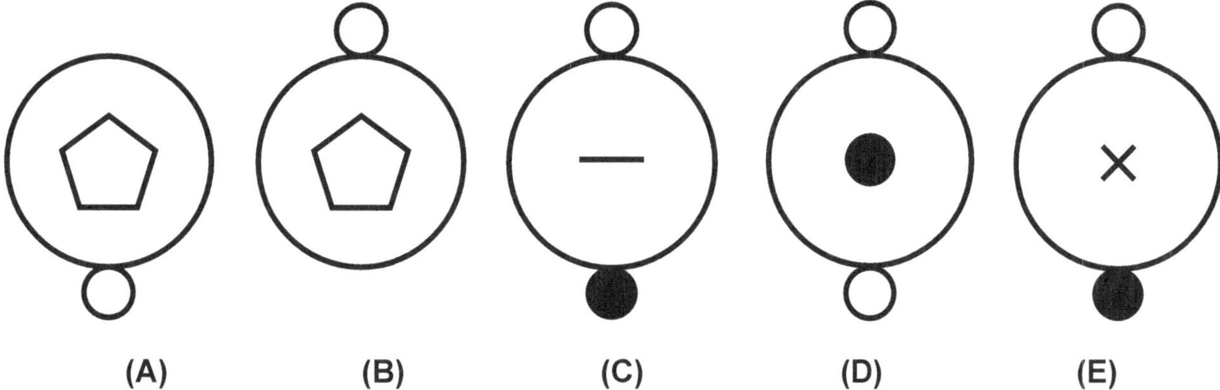

Question 7

Select the alternative that most logically and simply continues the series.

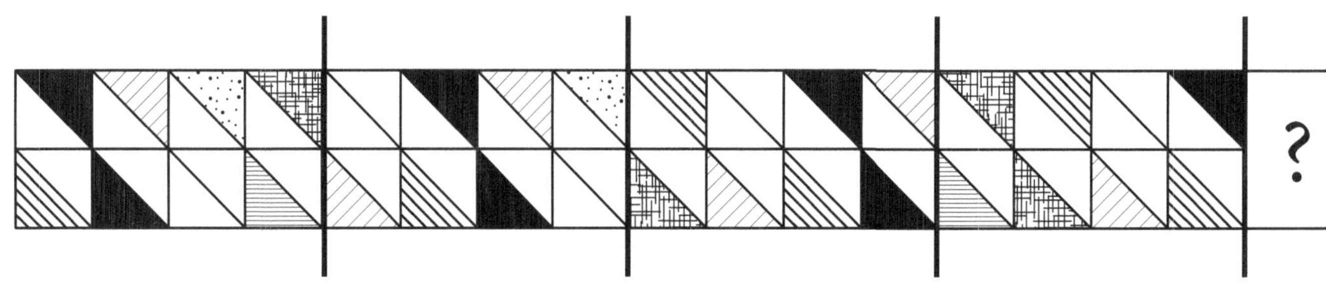

A) 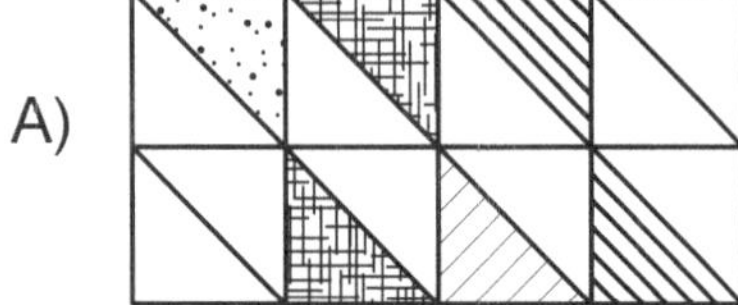

B) 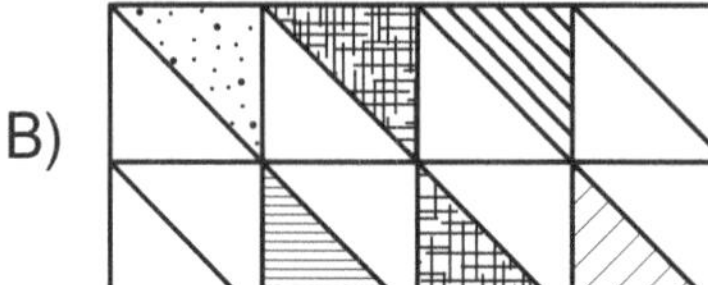

C) 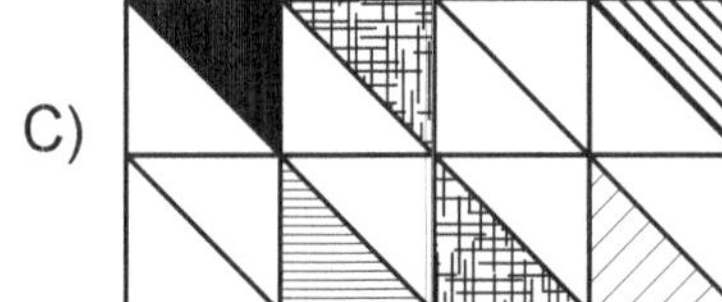

D) 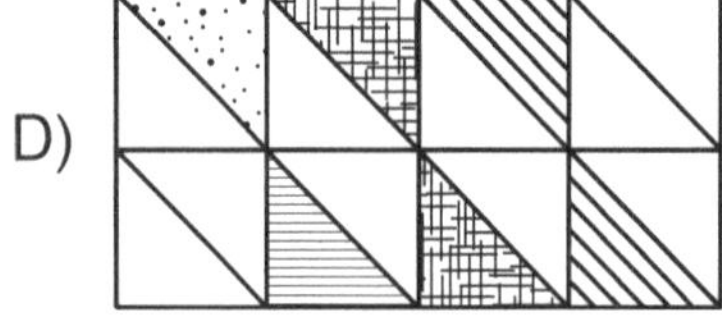

E) 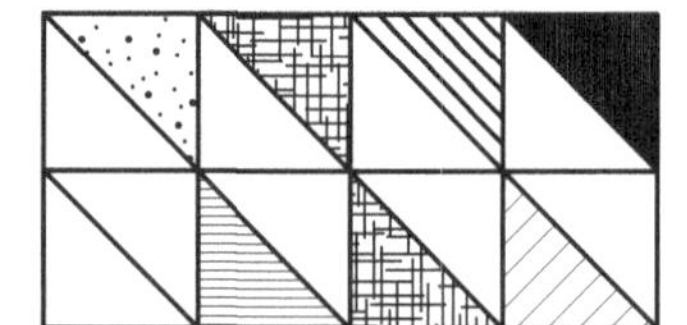

Question 8

Select the alternative that most logically and simply continues the series.

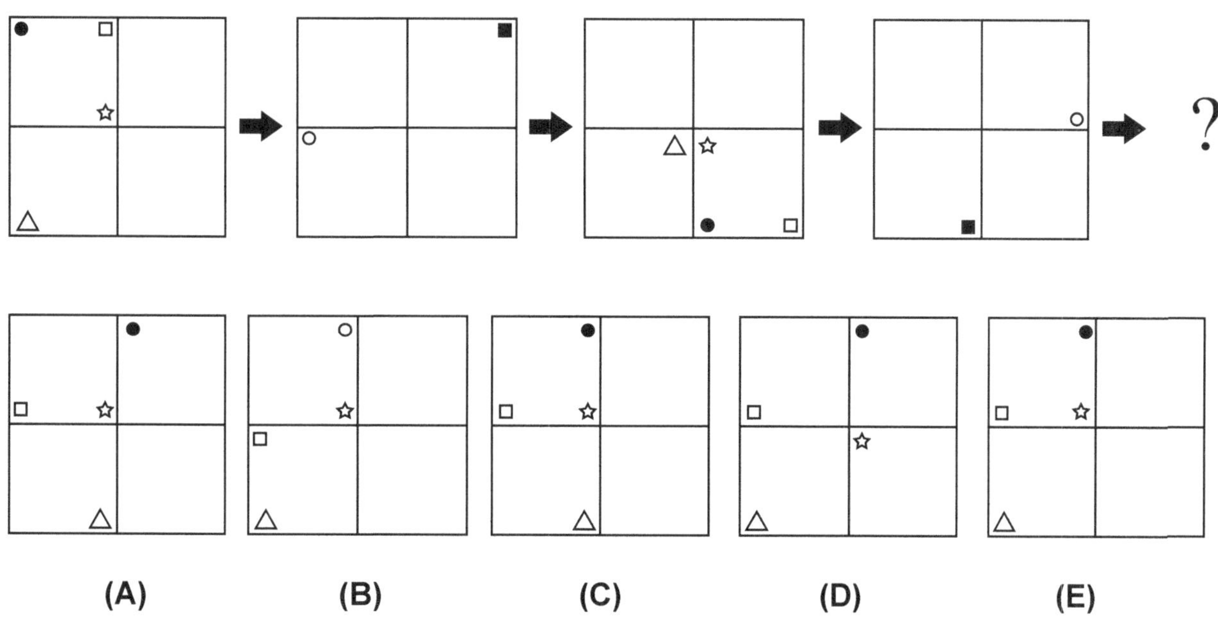

Question 9

Select the alternative that most logically and simply continues the series.

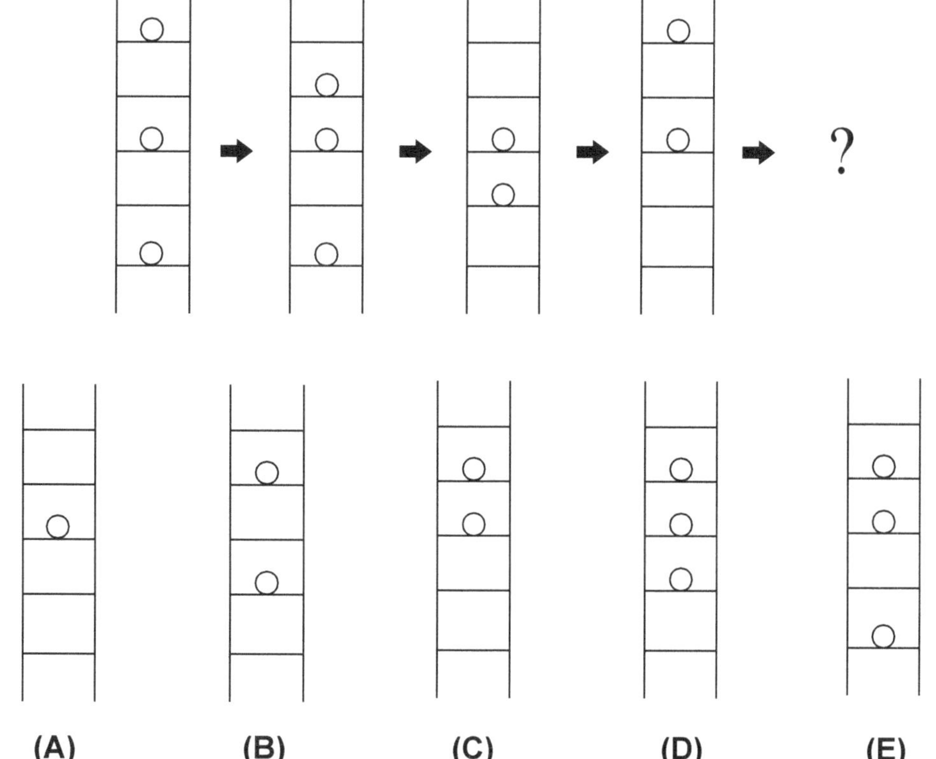

Question 10

Select the alternative that most logically and simply continues the series.

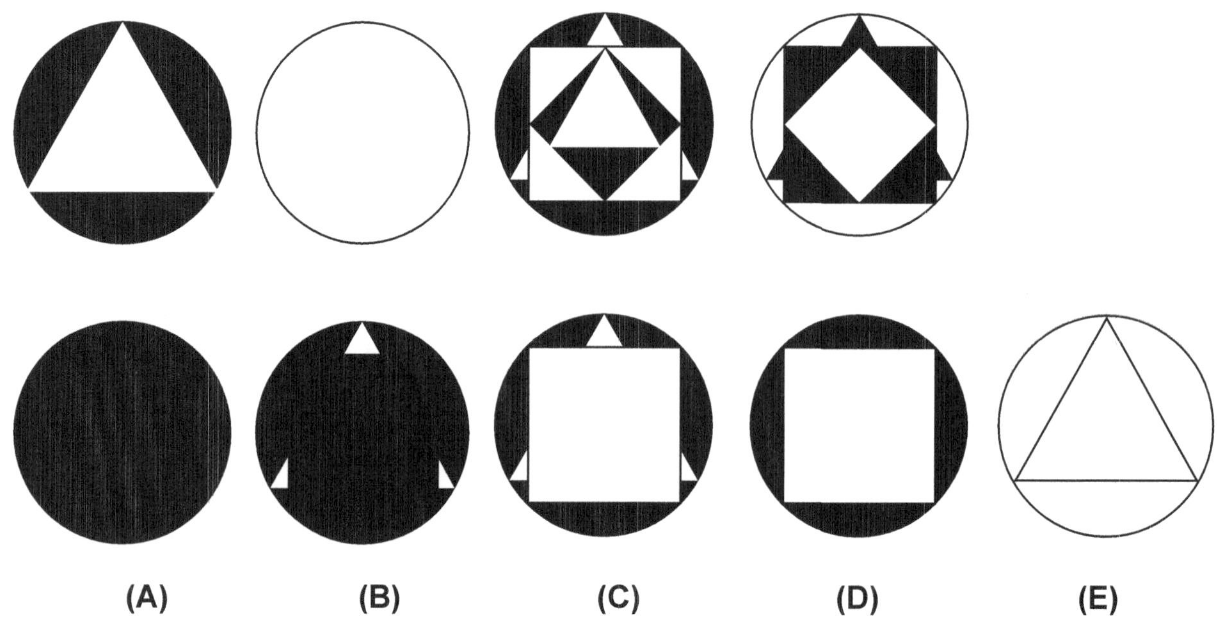

Question 11

Select the alternative that most logically and simply continues the series.

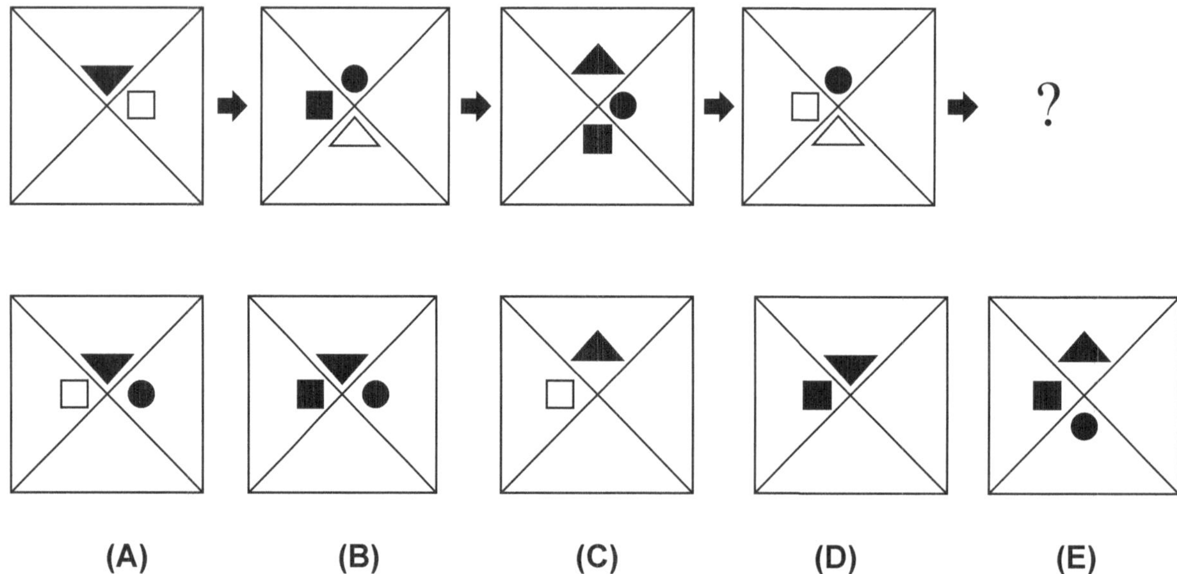

Question 12

Select the alternative that most logically and simply continues the series.

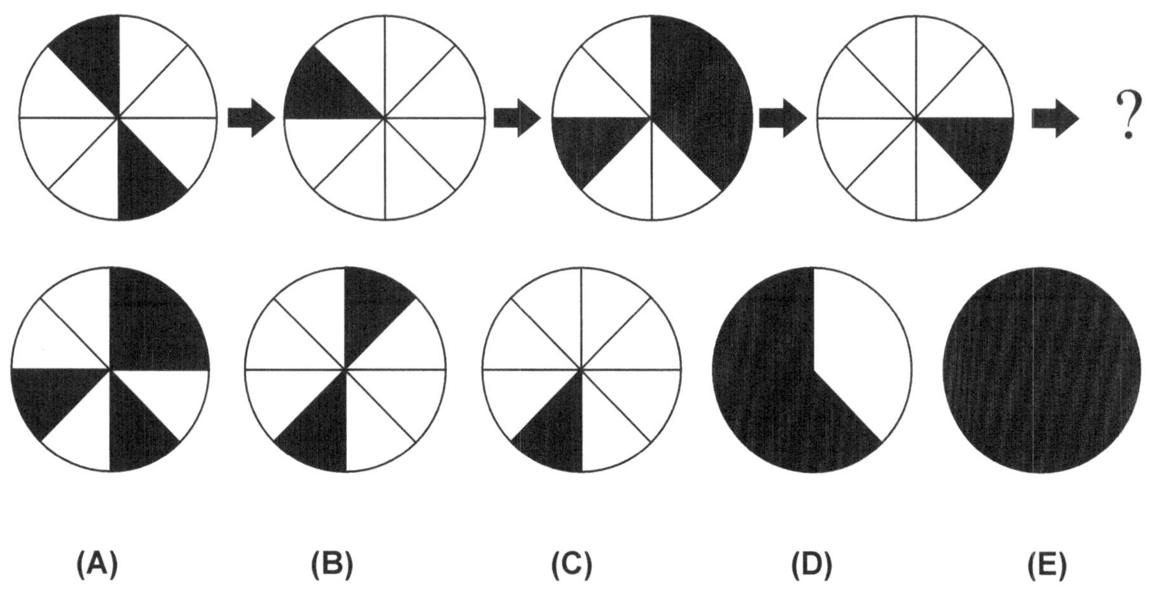

(A) (B) (C) (D) (E)

Question 13

Select the alternative that most logically and simply continues the series.

BUCYMJ	CTOBNL	DHZIFP	GQMBES

A) FWLVBC

B) KRLVBA

C) KRLVAB

D) FWLABE

E) KRLVBB

Question 14

Select the alternative that most logically and simply completes the picture.

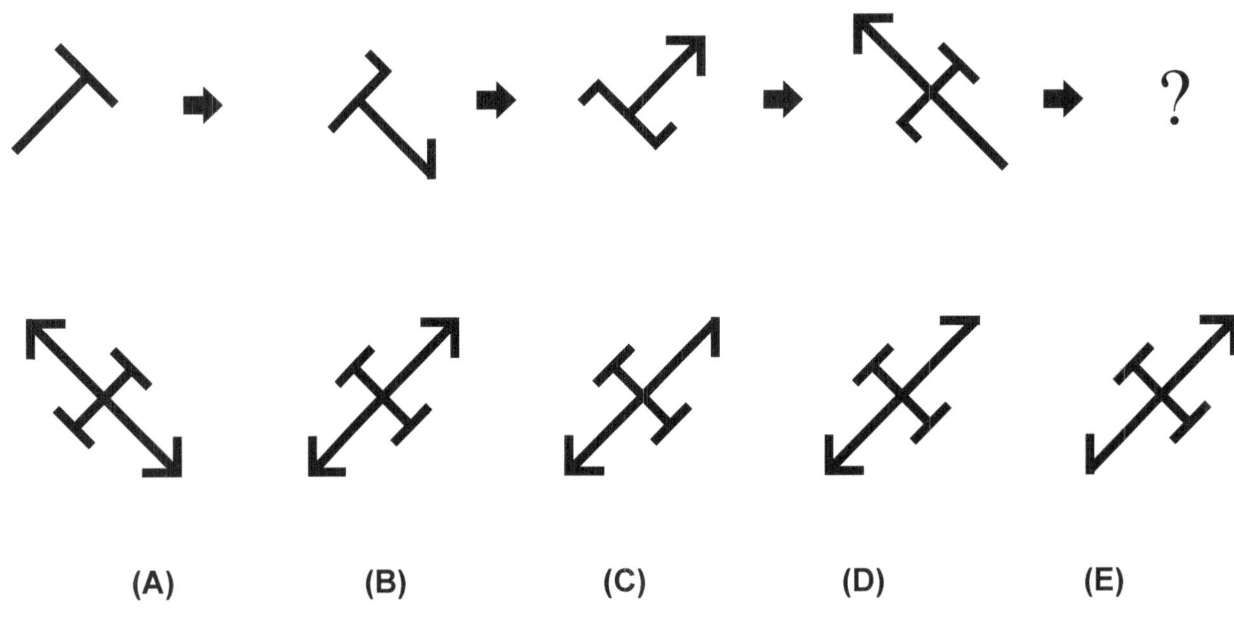

Question 15

Select the alternative that most logically and simply completes the picture.

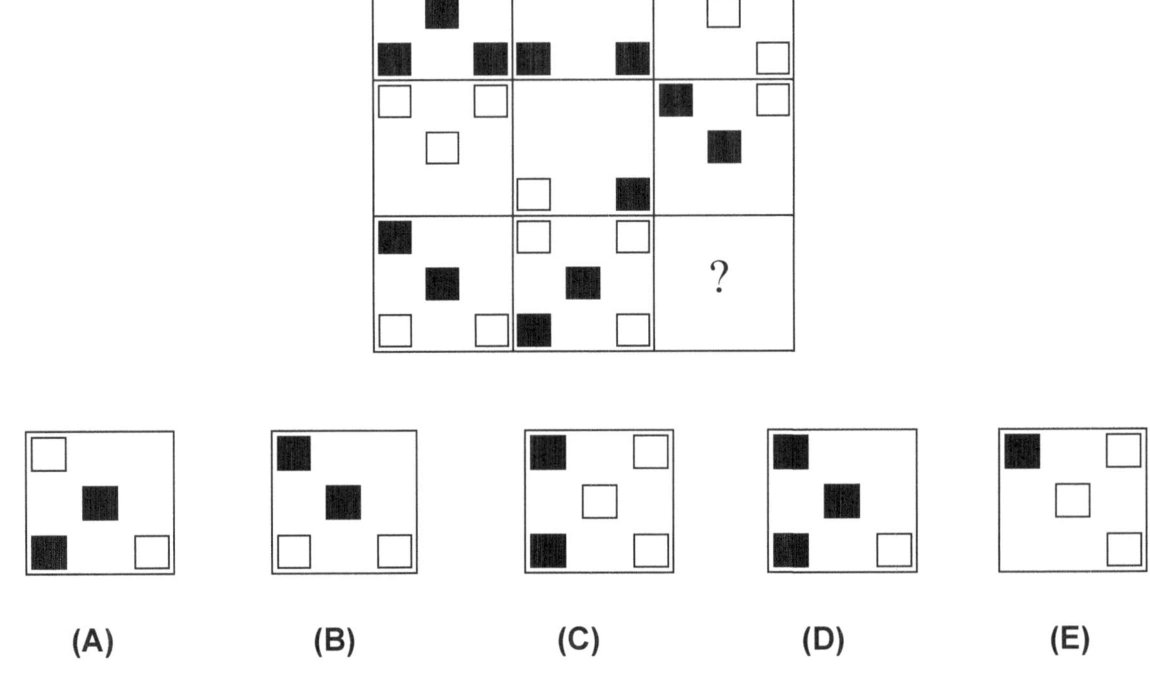

Question 16

Select the alternative that most logically and simply completes the picture.

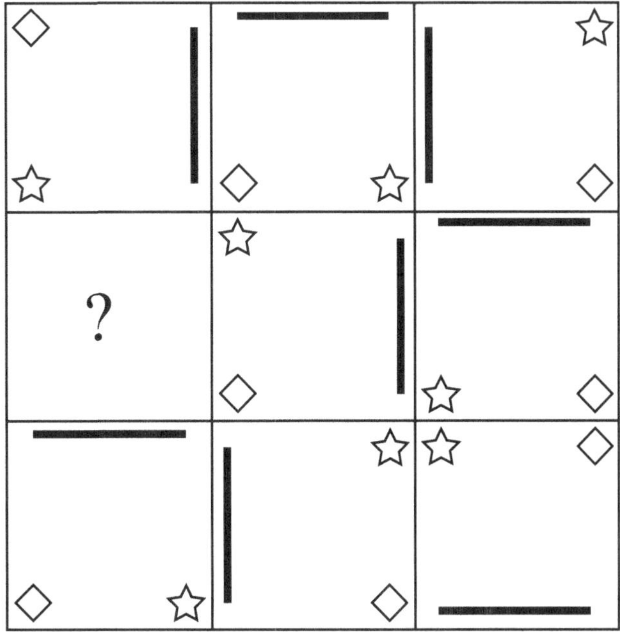

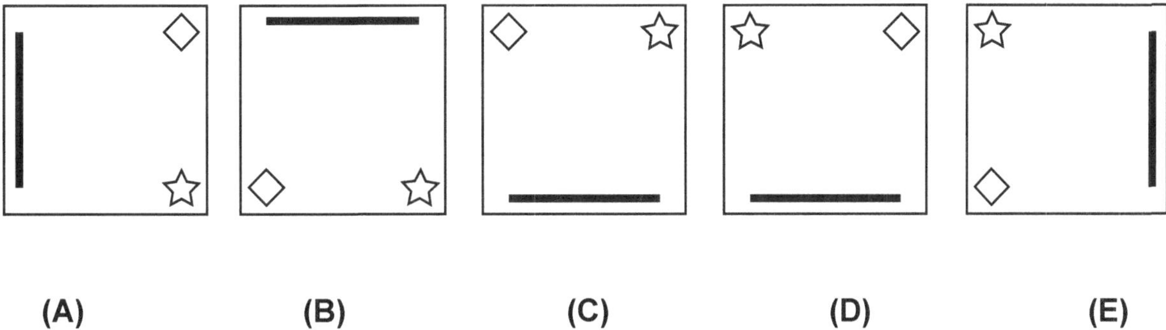

Question 17

Select the alternative that most logically and simply completes the picture.

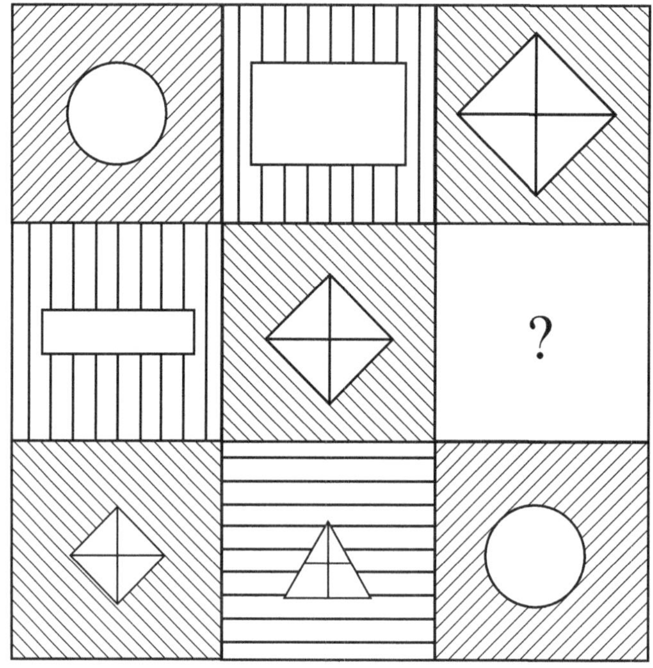

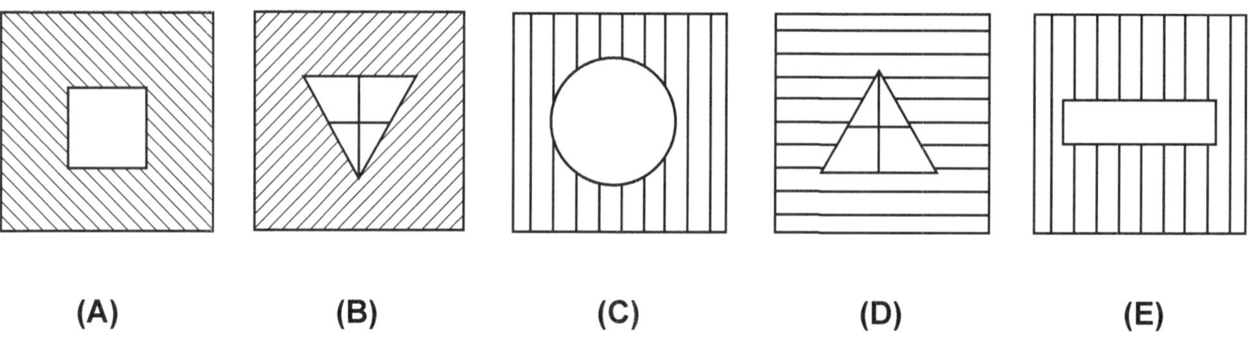

(A) (B) (C) (D) (E)

Question 18

Select the alternative that most logically and simply completes the picture.

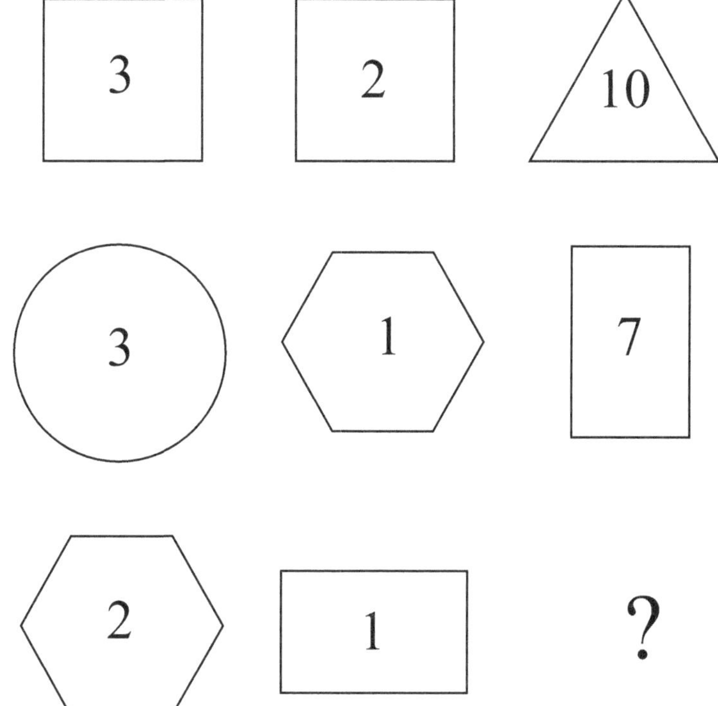

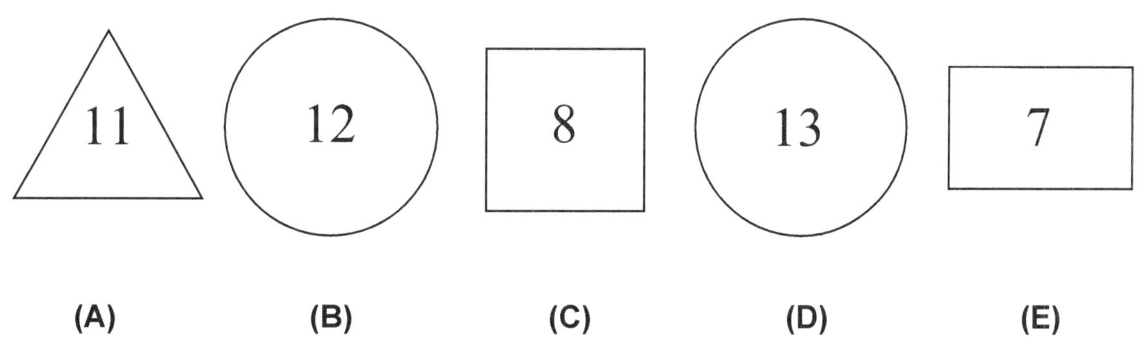

(A) (B) (C) (D) (E)

Question 19

Select the alternative that most logically and simply completes the picture.

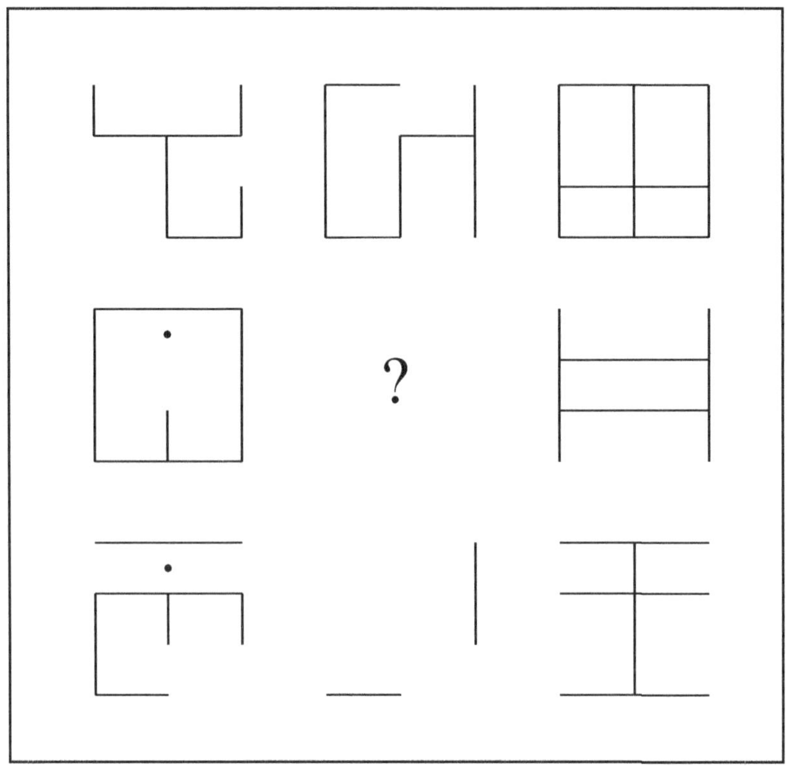

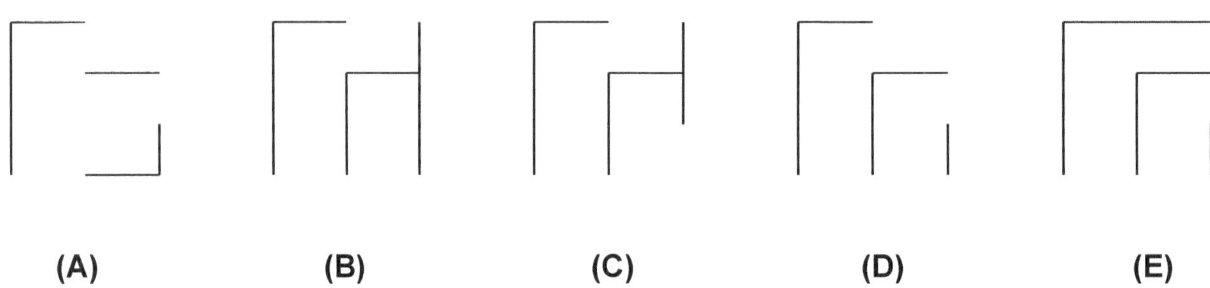

(A) (B) (C) (D) (E)

Question 20

Select the alternative that most logically and simply completes the picture.

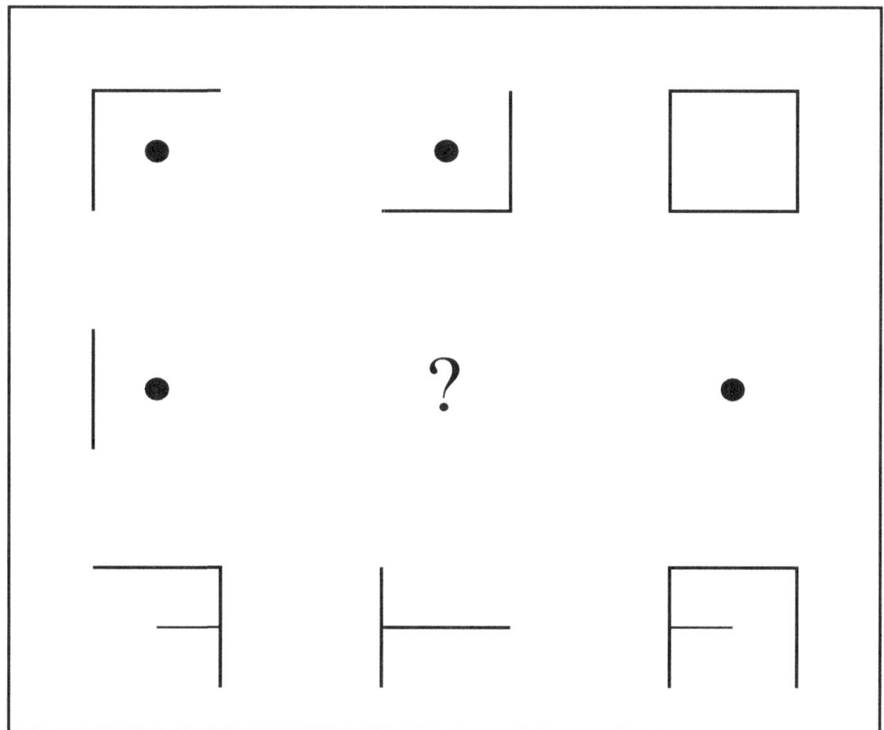

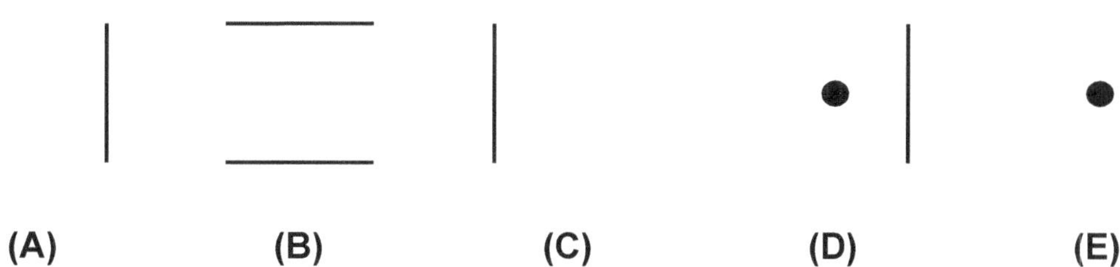

(A) (B) (C) (D) (E)

Question 21

Select the alternative that most logically and simply completes the picture.

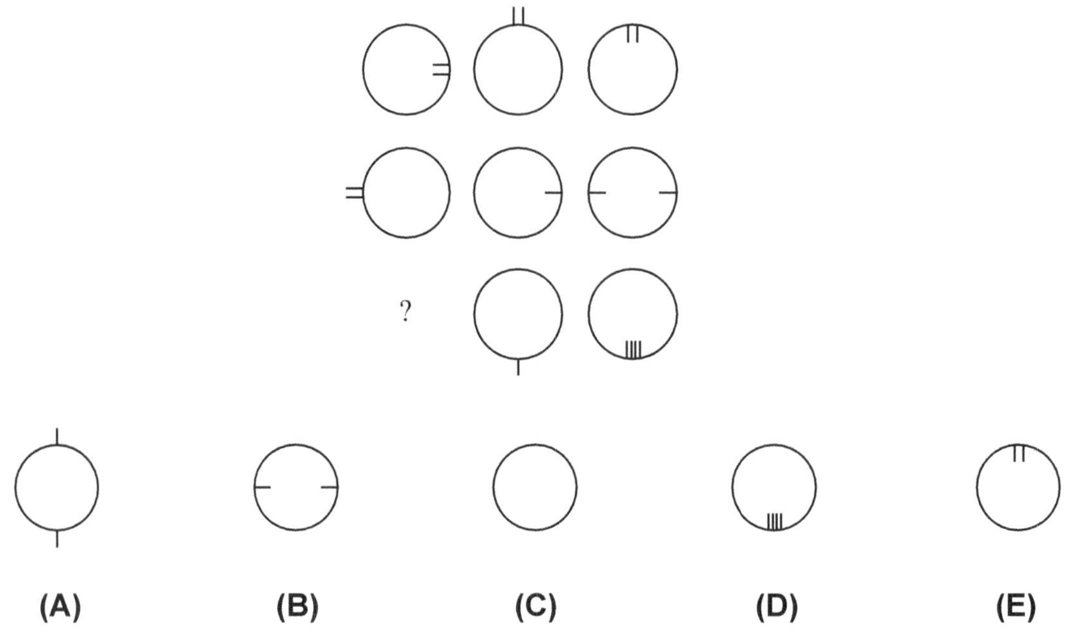

Question 22

Select the alternative that most logically and simply completes the picture.

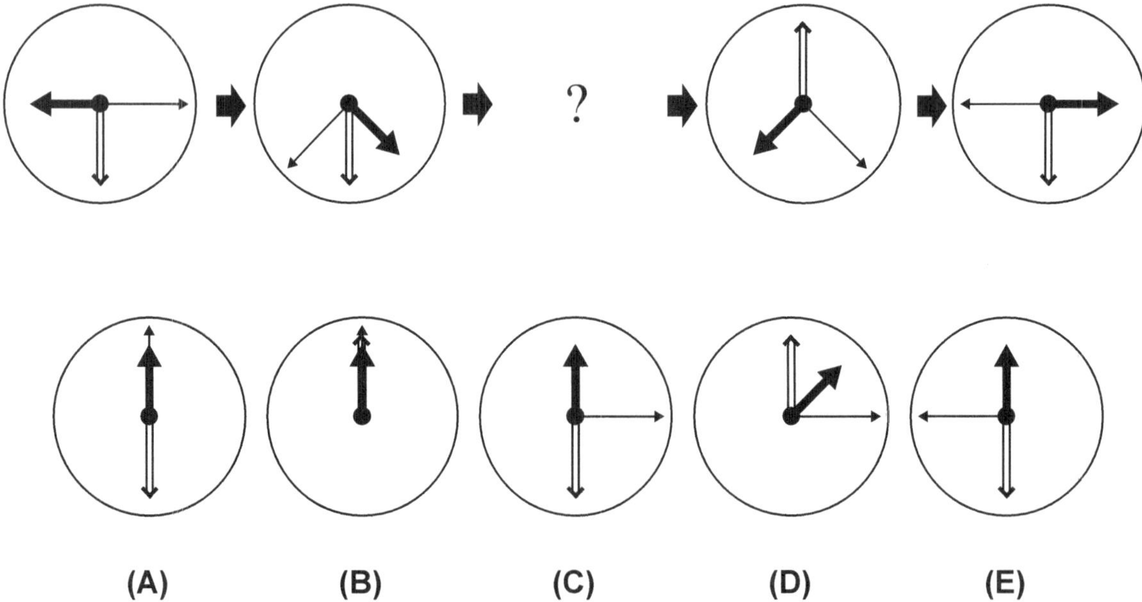

Question 23

Select the alternative that most logically and simply completes the picture.

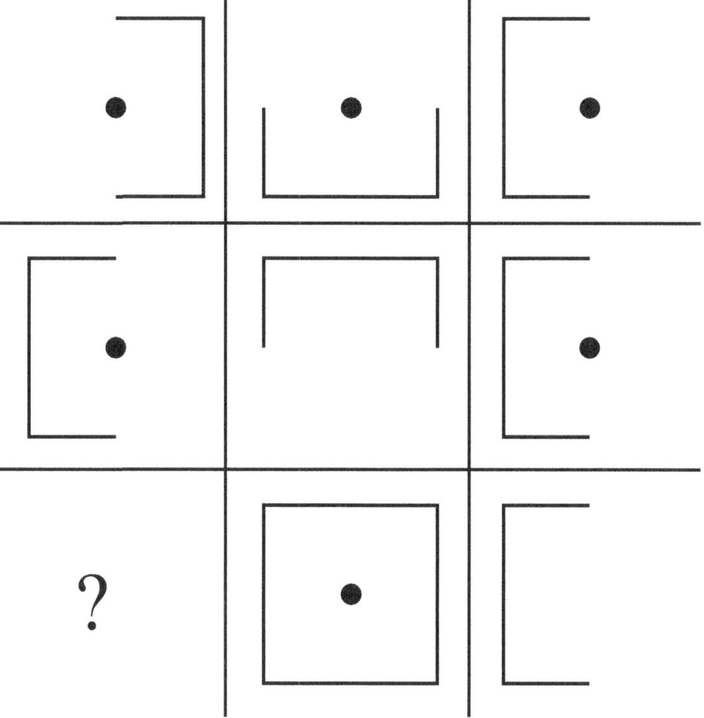

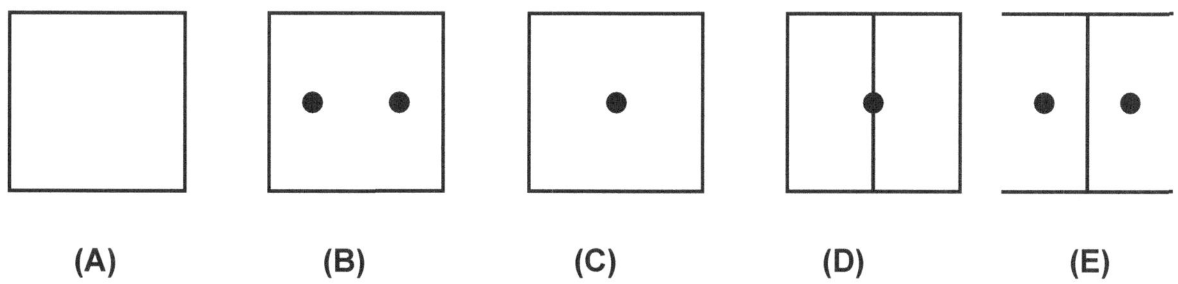

Question 24

Select the alternative that most logically and simply completes the picture.

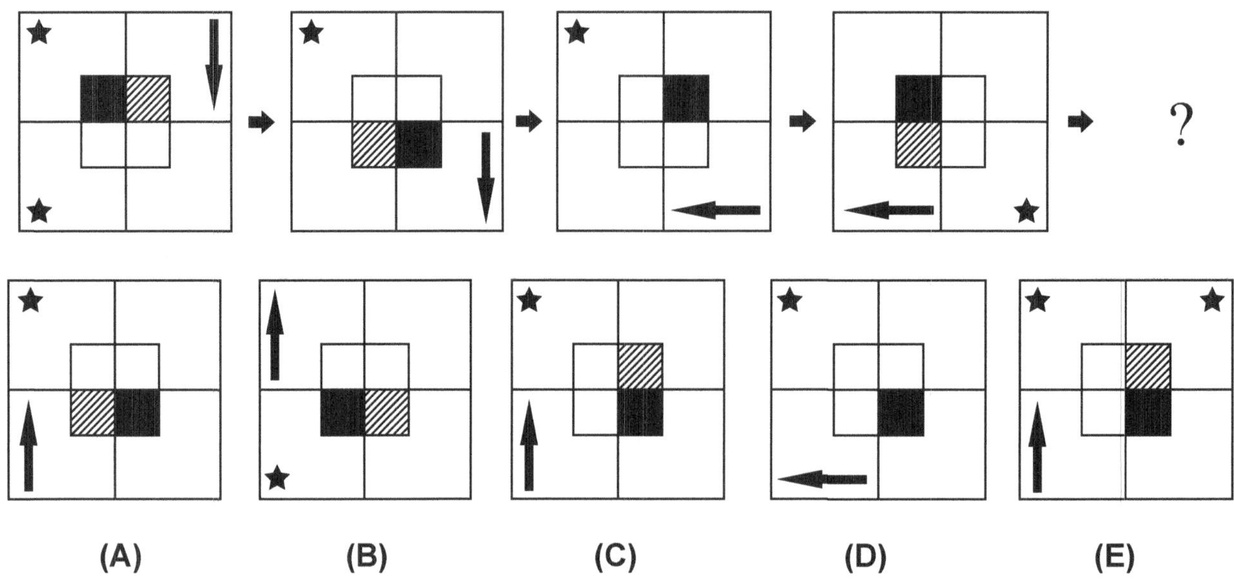

Question 25

Select the alternative that most logically and simply completes the picture.

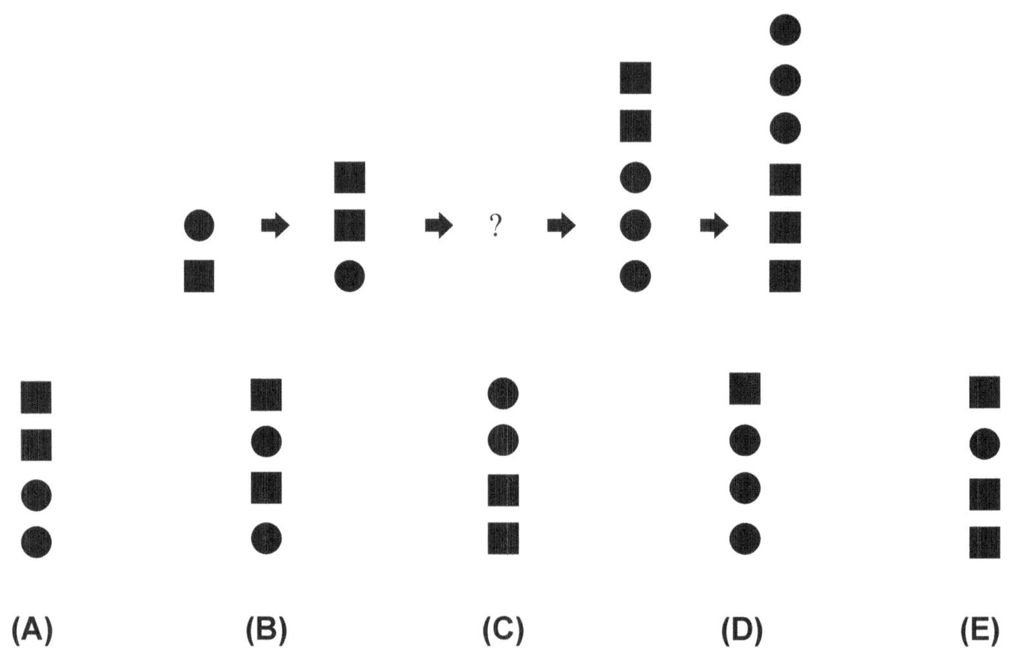

Question 26

Select the alternative that most logically and simply completes the picture.

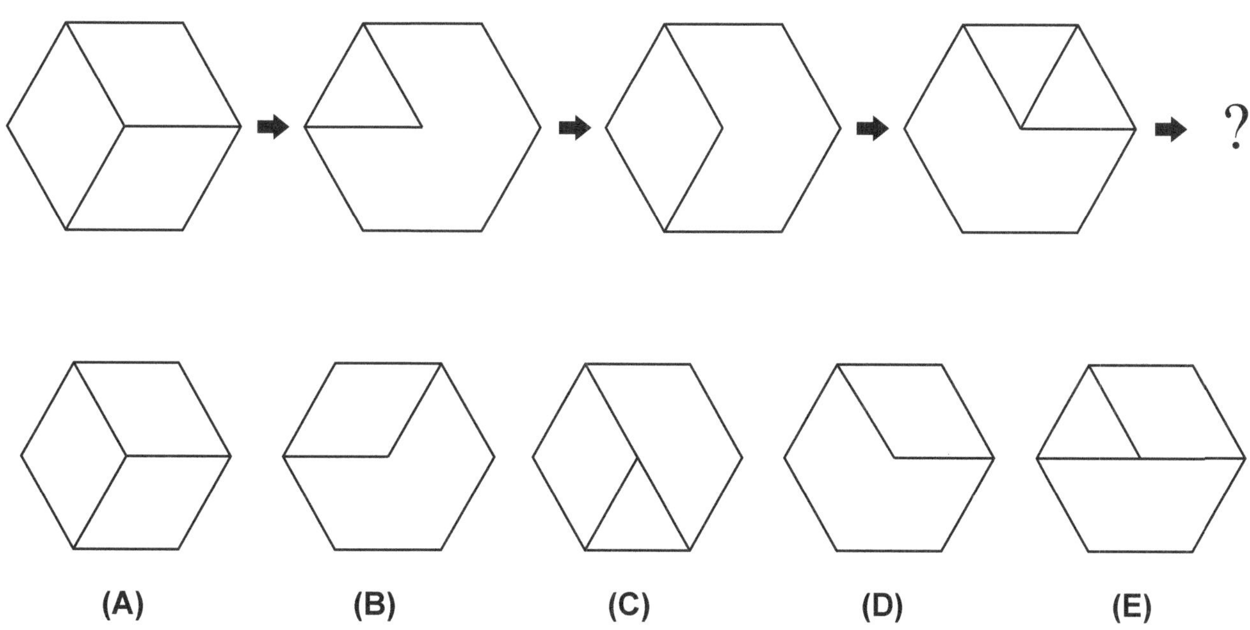

Question 27

Select the alternative that most logically and simply completes the picture.

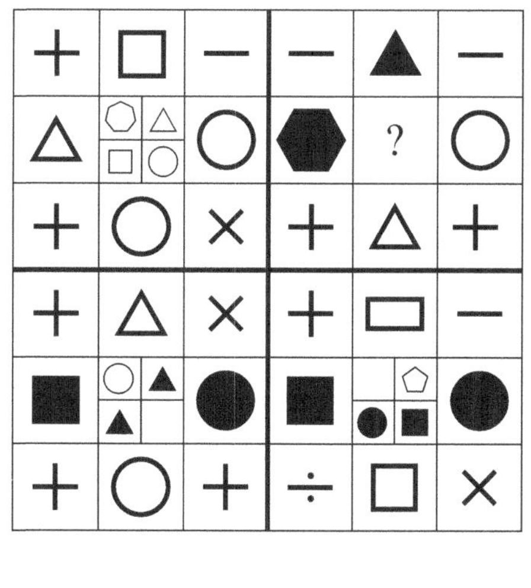

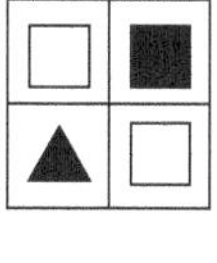

(A)

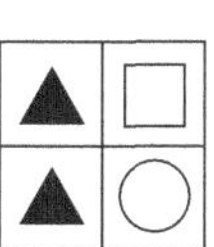

(B)

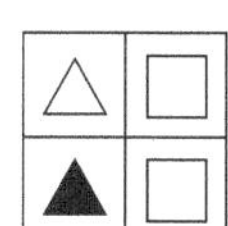

(C)

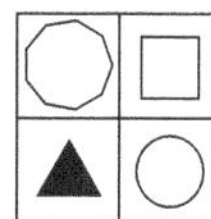

(D)

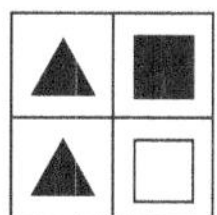

(E)

Question 28

Select the alternative that most logically and simply completes the picture.

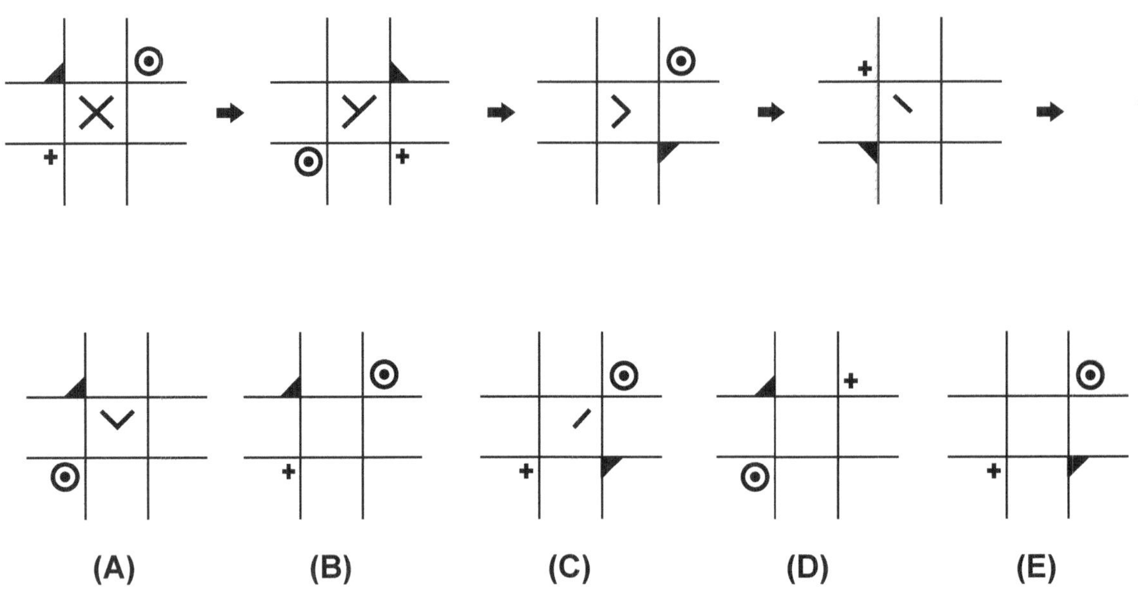

Question 29

In the question below, the five figures can be rearranged to form a logical sequence. Select the alternative that would most logically and simply be in the <u>middle</u> of the sequence.

ROABZV SOABZL RTAMZV SOABZV ROAMZV

ROABZV	ROAMZV	SOABZV	SOABZL	RTAMZV
(A)	(B)	(C)	(D)	(E)

Question 30

In the questions below, the five figures can be rearranged to form a logical sequence. Select the alternative that would most logically and simply be in the <u>middle</u> of the sequence.

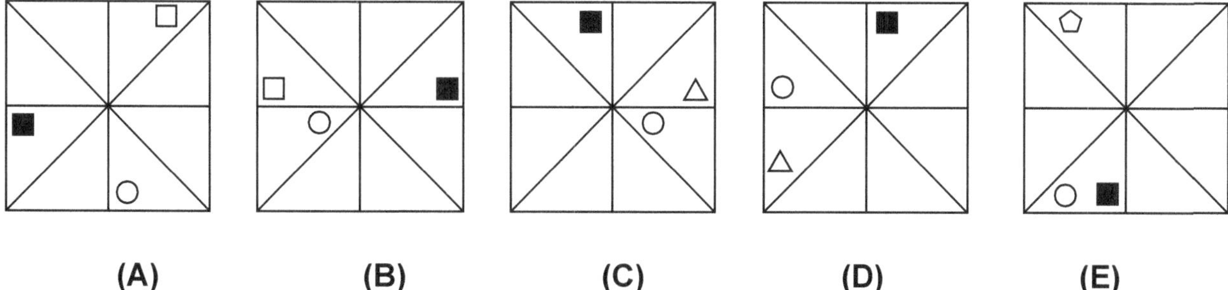

(A) (B) (C) (D) (E)

Question 31

In the questions below, the five figures can be rearranged to form a logical sequence. Select the alternative that would most logically and simply be in the <u>middle</u> of the sequence.

(A) (B) (C) (D) (E)

Question 32

In the question below, the five figures can be rearranged to form a logical sequence. Select the alternative that would most logically and simply be in the middle of the sequence.

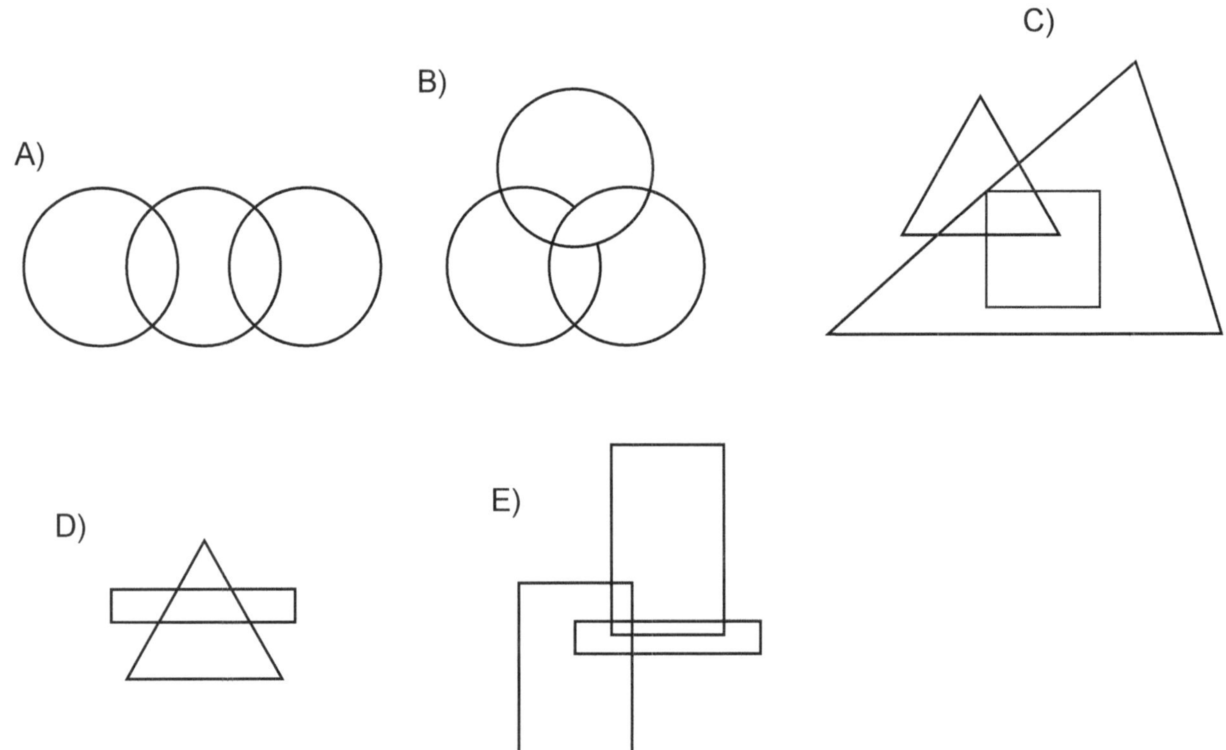

Question 33

In the questions below, the five figures can be rearranged to form a logical sequence. Select the alternative that would most logically and simply be in the <u>middle</u> of the sequence.

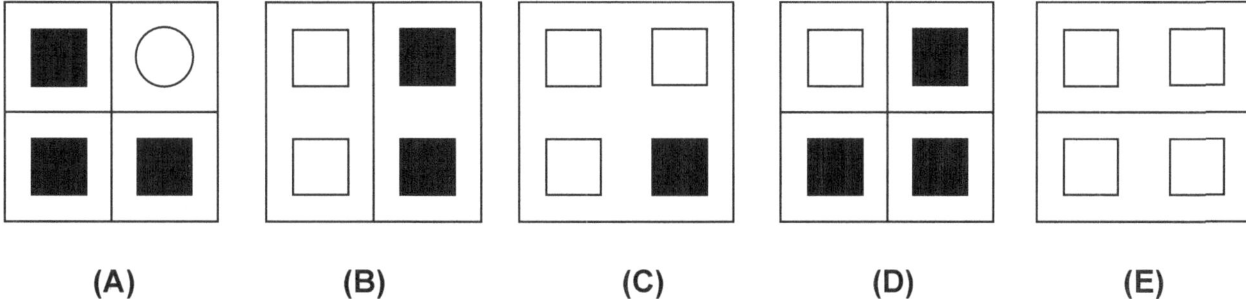

Question 34

In the questions below, the five figures can be rearranged to form a logical sequence. Select the alternative that would most logically and simply be in the <u>middle</u> of the sequence.

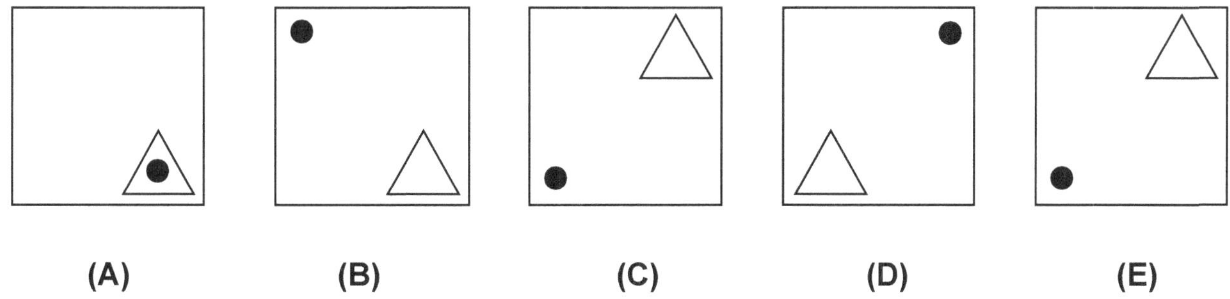

Question 35

In the questions below, the five figures can be rearranged to form a logical sequence. Select the alternative that would most logically and simply be in the <u>middle</u> of the sequence.

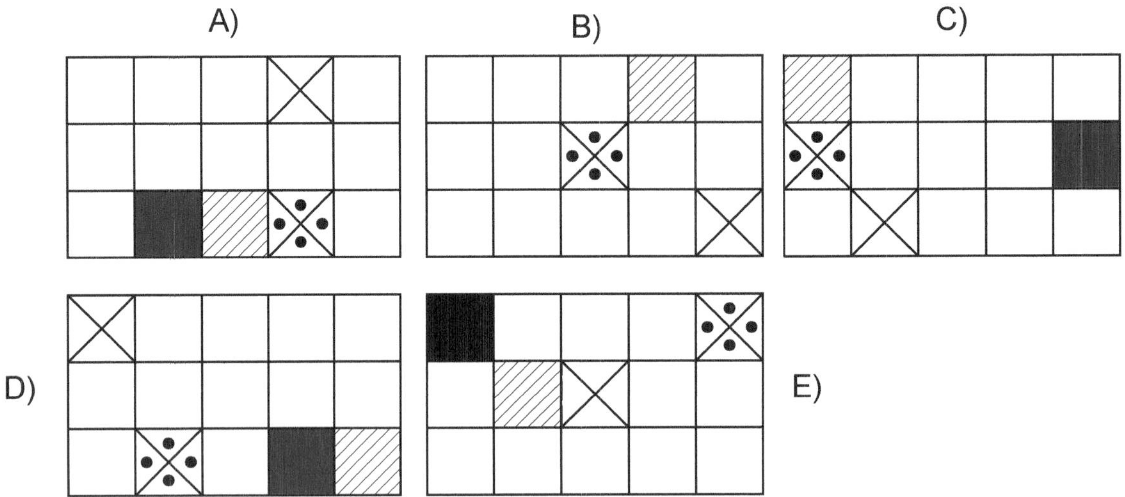

Question 36

In the questions below, the five figures can be rearranged to form a logical sequence. Select the alternative that would most logically and simply be in the middle of the sequence.

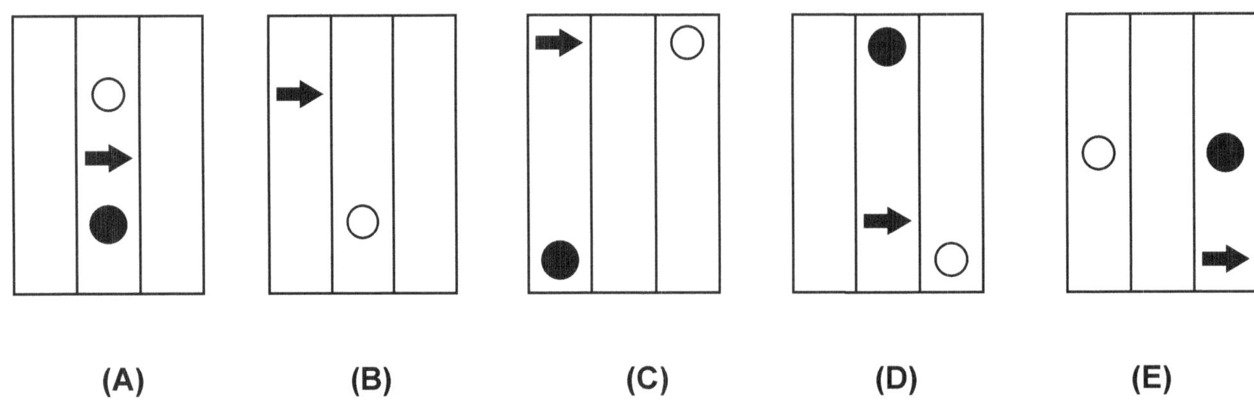

(A) **(B)** **(C)** **(D)** **(E)**

Question 37

In the questions below, the five figures can be rearranged to form a logical sequence.
Select the alternative that would most logically and simply be in the middle of the sequence.

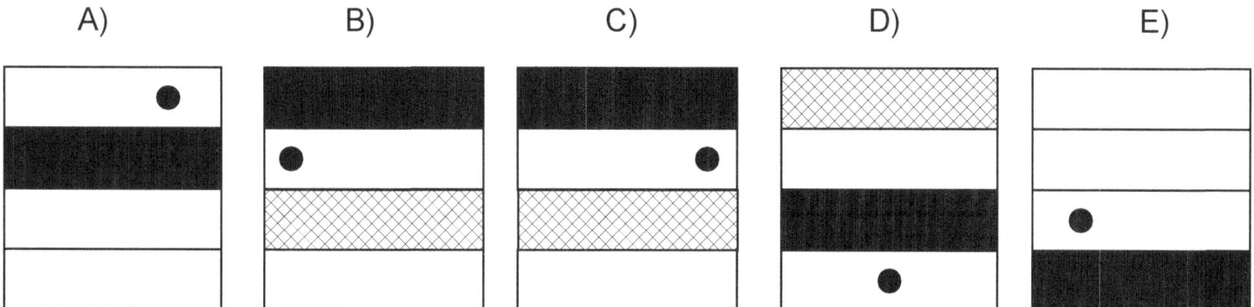

Question 38

In the questions below, the five figures can be rearranged to form a logical sequence.
Select the alternative that would most logically and simply be in the middle of the sequence.

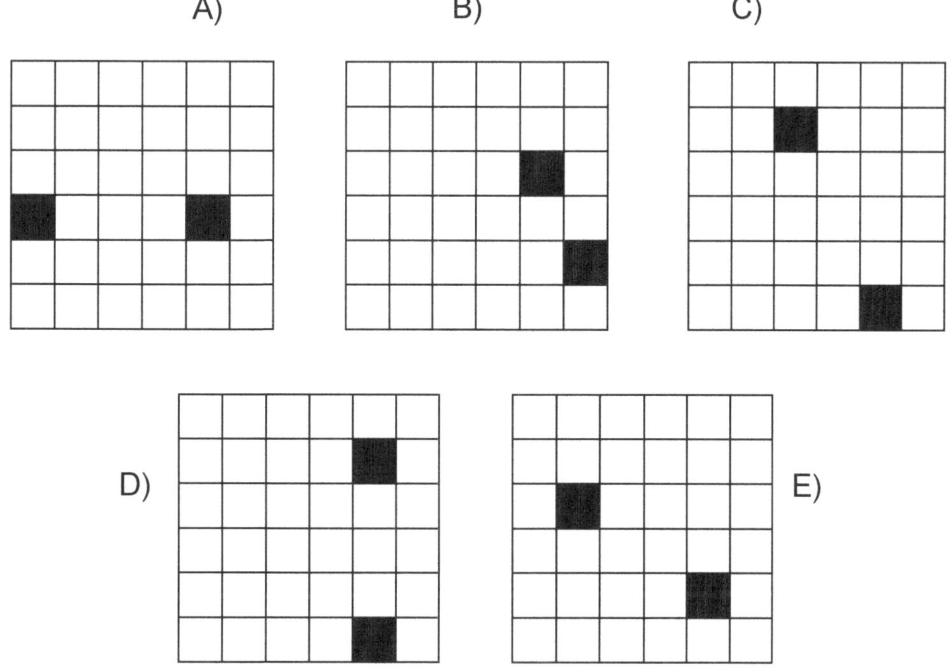

Question 39

In the questions below, the five figures can be rearranged to form a logical sequence.
Select the alternative that would most logically and simply be in the middle of the sequence.

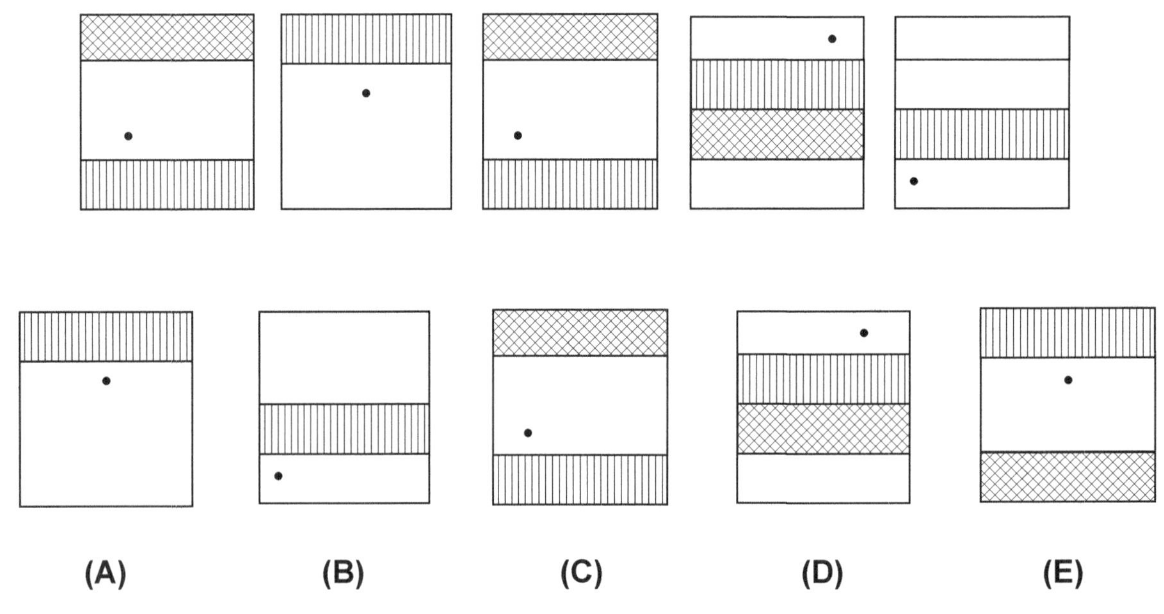

Question 40

In the questions below, the five figures can be rearranged to form a logical sequence.
Select the alternative that would most logically and simply be in the middle of the sequence.

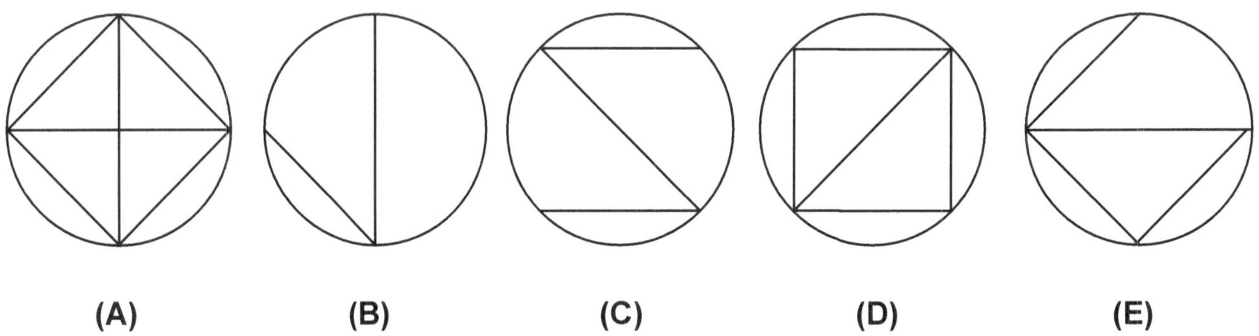

(A) (B) (C) (D) (E)

Question 41

In the questions below, the five figures can be rearranged to form a logical sequence. Select the alternative that would most logically and simply be in the middle of the sequence.

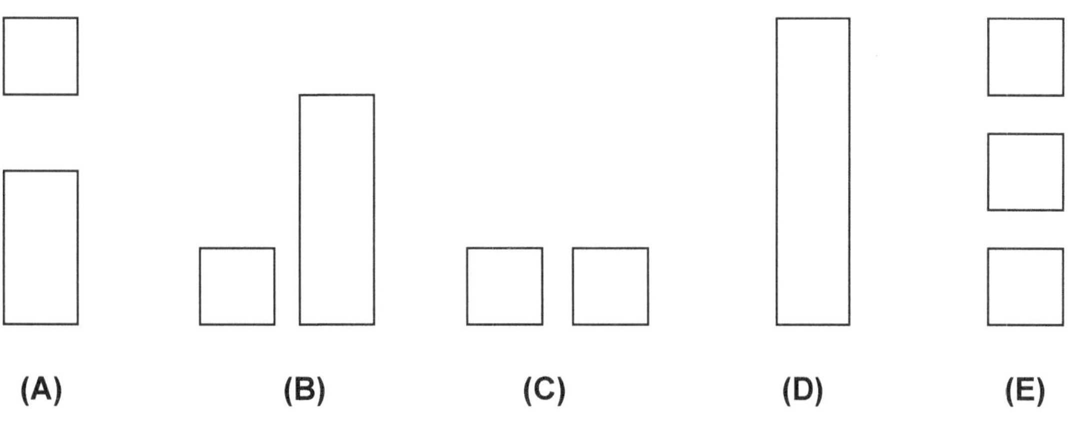

Question 42

In the questions below, the five figures can be rearranged to form a logical sequence. Select the alternative that would most logically and simply be in the middle of the sequence.

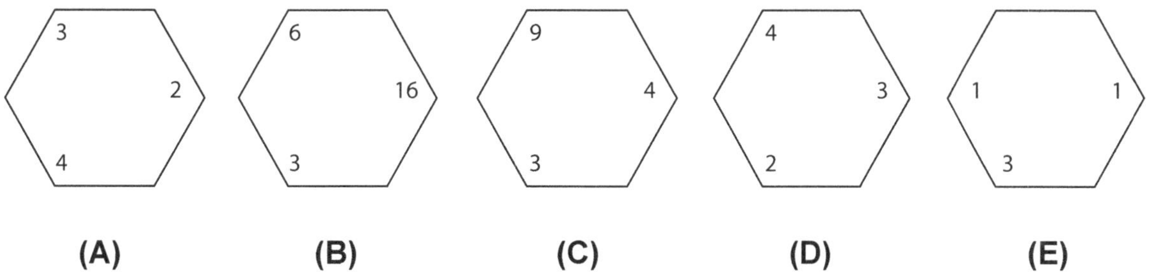

ANSWERS

Summary & Worked Solutions
Multiple Choice Answer Sheet

Summary of Answers

1	B	15	D	29	A
2	A	16	C	30	E
3	D	17	D	31	A
4	E	18	B	32	E
5	E	19	D	33	B
6	A	20	C	34	D
7	B	21	C	35	E
8	E	22	B	36	E
9	C	23	A	37	D
10	C	24	E	38	A
11	A	25	C	39	D
12	E	26	D	40	E
13	B	27	E	41	C
14	D	28	B	42	A

Worked Solutions

Question 1

B

Alternating pattern. Every second letter but not vowels – vowels for the first letter. Thus B is correct.

Question 2

A

Dot down two rungs. Double line up one rung – but hidden behind the single rung. Single line – up to rungs at a time. Scrolling misses a step and goes top to bottom or vice versa.

Question 3

D

Each of the first four shapes is made of 3 straight lines. Thus the next in order is K.

Question 4

E

Dot rotates anticlockwise two spaces, hence bottom left hand corner. The square alternates left and right. The x starts under the dot and moves clockwise one space at a time but is the hidden shape when anything else occupies the same space.

Question 5

E

The dot rotates anticlockwise one space, then two spaces, then three, then four. Thus it would be in the position shown in B, D and E. The triangle wedge goes clockwise two spaces twice, then backwards two spaces, twice, hence would be in the spot shown in B, C and E. The diamond moves from the inner circle to the outer circle and back, changing colour from black to white and moving clockwise. Thus it would be in the spot shown in B and E, but would be black not white, hence E is correct.

Question 6

A

The middle shape obtains an additional 'side' on each successive iteration, thus the middle shape must be a pentagon as in A or B. The small black dot alternates up and down and would thus it would be at the bottom. However, it is covered by the white dot, which has rotated outside to inside, but changes direction from clockwise to anticlockwise – thus A is correct.

B cannot be correct as the black dot is missing.

Question 7

B

The shapes on the top row move left to right one space at a time. The shapes in the lower row also move left to right one space at a time – thus looking carefully, B is correct. Note – the bottom right-hand shape is the one to look at very carefully.

Question 8

E

The dot moves anticlockwise and changes from black to white and vice versa thus C or D must be correct. The square rotates clockwise and also changes colour from white to black and vice versa and so would be in the position shown in C. The white triangle is rotating clockwise one space at a time but is sometimes hidden by another shape. The star is alternating across the middle but skips every second shape.

Question 9

C

The middle ball is staying still. The top ball moves up one place scrolling to the bottom. The bottom ball move up three places, scrolling to the bottom after reaching the top. Hence, C is correct.

Question 10

C

There are 5 shapes – in order a small triangle, a diamond, a large square, a large triangle and the circle. The circle alternates from black to white and thus must be black. The triangle also alternates but from white to black and thus must be white. The square, hidden underneath in the first two pictures, alternates colour and thus should be white as well. Hence C is correct.

Question 11

A

There are two alternating patterns, thus the first and third pictures follow a pattern and the second a fourth do. In this case, looking at the first and third pattern it can be seen that the black triangle is flipping over and thus should be back to pointing downwards as shown in A, B or D. The square is rotating anticlockwise by one space and changing colour – so in the next picture it should be white and in the position shown in A and C. Finally, the dot does not move, but was uncovered when the square moved. Thus the correct answer for all three icons must be A.

Question 12

E

The pattern here is 2 out of eight shaded, then one out of eight, then four, then one, then all eight. That is 2^1, 2^0, 2^2, 2^0, 2^3. Hence E is correct. The relationship between the shading is powers of 2.

Question 13

B

Watch the movement of the vowels (from U – O – I – E – ?) as the shift in the otherwise random arrangement of letters from 2nd, to 3rd to 4th to 5th position. Thus, in the answer the letter A should be at the end as shown in B.

Question 14

D

Look carefully – there are TWO changes with each successive iteration of the picture. Moreover, there is 90° anti-clockwise rotation thus eliminating A and E as possibilities. The answer cannot however be B as this involves three changes (the arrowhead and the extension of one wing). Out of C and D, D is correct as the correct side of the arrow (as per second picture) emerges.

Question 15

D

The key here is as follows (adding downwards the top row onto the second row):

Black square + white square = black square
White square + nothing = white square
White square + white square = nothing
Black square + nothing = white square
Black square + black square = white square
Nothing + nothing = black square

Applying this key means that there should be a black square in the top left hand corner and in the middle, a white square in the bottom right hand corner, nothing in the top right corner and a black square in the bottom left hand corner. This is shown in answer D.

Question 16

C

The shapes each rotate one place anti clockwise across each row. Thus, moving each shape clockwise one space from the middle figure would give the positions shown in answer C.

Question 17

D

The shapes get successively smaller if you follow the diagonals right to left.

Question 18

B

The sum of the number in the middle and the sides of the shape are added across the rows. Thus in the first row, 3 + 4 (number of sides of a square) + 2 + 4 (square) = 13 (or 10 +3 – number of sides in a triangle).

Similarly, in the second row 3 + 1 (circle) + 1 + 6 (hexagon) = 11 = 7 + 4 (number of sides in a rectangle).
Hence in the bottom row: 2 + 6 (hexagon) + 1 + 4 (rectangle) = 13 (or 12 + 1 (circle) as in B.
Note that: A equals 14, C = 12, D = 14 and E =11.

Question 19

D

In each column the sum of the top and bottom shapes equals the middle shape. However, there is a trick – each overlapping line disappears. Thus, the answer must be D.

Question 20

C

In each row the shapes add across left to right. However, overlapping shapes, line or dots disappear. Thus the correct answer must be C.

Question 21

C

The circles add downwards, with lines outside denoting positive numbers and lines inside the circles denoting negative numbers. Thus, in the middle column: 2 + -1 = 1 and in the right hand column -2 + -2 = -4. Thus in the left hand column -2 + 2 = 0 hence C is correct.

Question 22

B

The long minute hand is at the "6" for two pictures, then rotates to the 12 for 2 pictures whilst changing to black. Hence only C and D can be correct. The hour hand move anticlockwise (or counter rotates) 135 degrees at a time and thus must be also pointing to the 12. The second hand rotates by 135 degrees clockwise and thus would be at the 12. Hence at the hands point upwards to the 12 simultaneously, as shown in B.

Question 23

A

The shapes add downwards, and overlapping lines DO NOT disappear. However, overlapping dots DO disappear. Hence the answer must be A.

Question 24

E

There is alternating pattern here. The first, third and fifth diagrams are related, as are the second and fourth. So, what exactly is occurring? The star in the top left hand corner of the outer square does not move. In terms of the inner four squares, the top right one (with angled lines also never changes). Thus, only three things change – the black square rotates clockwise by one space, the bottom left hand star also rotates clockwise by one space in the outer squares and the arrow moves clockwise by one square at a time. Thus E is correct.

Question 25

C

The pattern of dots swap places in each successive picture thus in the missing set the squares must be at the bottom. Moreover, there is an addition to the shapes on the bottom each time, hence the correct answer must be two black squares at the bottom and two black circles at the top. Thus, C is correct.

Question 26

D

Watch the three lines carefully. The one from the middle of the hexagon to the right, rotates anticlockwise two positions on each occasion. The line pointing downwards to the left rotates clockwise one space at a time, while the third line, pointing to the top left – never moves. Following this pattern gives the movement of lines denoted in D.

Question 27

E

This is a mathematical question, done through the use of shapes. A black shape denotes a negative number equivalent in value to the number of lines associated with the shape. A white shape denotes a positive number equivalent to the number of lines associated with the shape. The mathematical rules are to start at the top of each set of nine and 'do' the operation. Hence, looking at the bottom right hand group of nine squares and starting with the white rectangle (or number 4) this is to subtract negative 1 (black circle) giving five (denoted by the pentagon in the adjacent middle square. Moving around, the black circle (-1) multiples by +4 equals -4 (the small black square in the middle. Moving to the next operation we have 4 (white square) being divided by -4 (black square) to give -1 (black circle) and then we have -4 (black square) add to 4 (white rectangle) to give zero (denoted by an empty box).

Following these rules and applying them to the missing group would give the following middle squares: -3 (black triangle) – 1 (white circle) should give -4 (a black square). Next we have +1 (white circle) + 3 (white triangle) = +4 (white square). At the bottom we have +3 (white triangle) + -6 (black hexagon) = -3 (black triangle).
Lastly, -6 – (-3) = -3 (or black triangle). Thus the correct answer must be E.

Question 28

B

The black triangle move clockwise one corner at time and thus should be back where it begun. The circle and dot keeps alternating between the top right hand corner and bottom left corner – but can be hidden. The plus sign is moving counter clockwise one space at a time, but is hidden in the third figure by the circle and dot. Finally, the middle shape is losing one 'arm' at a time and thus the middle square will be empty in the fifth iteration.

Question 29

A

Start at any arrangement of letters and place below it the group of letters that is one letter different Thus, RTAMZV will have ROAMZV below it. This would then have ROABZV below it and below that would be SOABZV. Finally there would be SOABZL. This will give the correct sequence regards of the sequence one start with – if there is no sequence with one letter different in one direction then it represents the end of the changes. Just go above instead of below. Hence the middle sequence of letters in order is ROABZV or A.

Question 30

E

The key here is the clear shape as it moves counter clockwise. It goes from 3-sided (C) to 4-sided (A) to 5-sided (E) to 4-sided (B) to 3-sided (D). Hence the middle shape is E.

Question 31

A

The number of hydrogen atoms goes from 2 – 3 – 4 – 3 – 2. Hence the answer must be A.

Question 32

E

The number of shapes in TOTAL caused by the overlapping shapes rises from 5 (A) to 6 (B) to 7 (E), then back to 6 (C) and 5 (D). Hence E must be correct.

Question 33

B

Start with four white squares and one line (E). This becomes 3 white squares and one black square and no line (C). Then it becomes two white squares and two black squares with one line (B), three black squares and one white square with two lines (D) and finishes with three black squares, a white circle and 2 lines.

Question 34

D

The white triangle must start and finish in the top right hand corner. It then goes clockwise one space (twice) and then back. Hence the sequence is E-B-D-A to C. Hence the middle shape is D.

Question 35

E

The sequence is D-C-E-A-B (note each of the shapes is moving on the diagonal and scrolling).

Question 36

E

The arrow is moving downwards two spaces and rightwards one space each time. It starts as in C. The white ball is falling from the top right hand corner downwards and leftwards until the position in E, then move down and right. The black ball move upwards and right, but in the fourth picture is behind the arrow. Hence the pattern is: C – A – E – B – D and the middle of the sequence is E – again!

Question 37

D

The dot appears to be starting at the left (as in B) and falling downwards one row at a time whilst moving left to right. The black row is moving upwards one row at a time and scrolling from the top to the bottom. The cross hatched row is moving downwards by one row at a time but is masked by the black row when they coincide. Hence the sequence is: B – E – D – A – C and D is in the middle.

Question 38

A

The bottom right hand square in D moves upwards one space each time, hence the sequence is C – E – A – B – D. The other dark square is moving downwards to the left one space each time.

Question 39

D

The row with vertical lines move upwards one row at a time. The black dot moves downwards to the left and scrolls. The row with the cross-hatched lines is rising one row at a time but will 'disappear' if it falls onto a row where the dot appears. Hence the sequence is: A – E – D – B – C and D is in the middle.

Question 40

E

Here we are adding one line each time and rotating the shape counter-clockwise by 90 degrees each time. Hence the sequence is B – C – E – D – A with E being in the middle.

Question 41

C

This is simply based on an equivalent number of squares: A = 3, B = 4, C = 2, D = 4 and E = 3. Hence the middle must be 2 or C.

Question 42

A

The key here is to follow the squares (2^2, 1^2, 2^2, 3^2, 4^2) that rotates clockwise two spaces each time. Hence the order is: D – E – A – C – B and the middle of the sequence is A.

Notes

Notes

Notes

Notes

Notes

Notes

Essential Preparation for

UMAT

UNDERGRADUATE MEDICINE & HEALTH SCIENCES ADMISSION TEST

MULTIPLE CHOICE ANSWER SHEET

Use pencil when filling out this sheet

Fill in the circle correctly				
●	B	C	D	E

If you make a mistake neatly cross it out and circle the correct response				
✕	●	C	D	E

1	A	B	C	D	E	22	A	B	C	D	E
2	A	B	C	D	E	23	A	B	C	D	E
3	A	B	C	D	E	24	A	B	C	D	E
4	A	B	C	D	E	25	A	B	C	D	E
5	A	B	C	D	E	26	A	B	C	D	E
6	A	B	C	D	E	27	A	B	C	D	E
7	A	B	C	D	E	28	A	B	C	D	E
8	A	B	C	D	E	29	A	B	C	D	E
9	A	B	C	D	E	30	A	B	C	D	E
10	A	B	C	D	E	31	A	B	C	D	E
11	A	B	C	D	E	32	A	B	C	D	E
12	A	B	C	D	E	33	A	B	C	D	E
13	A	B	C	D	E	34	A	B	C	D	E
14	A	B	C	D	E	35	A	B	C	D	E
15	A	B	C	D	E	36	A	B	C	D	E
16	A	B	C	D	E	37	A	B	C	D	E
17	A	B	C	D	E	38	A	B	C	D	E
18	A	B	C	D	E	39	A	B	C	D	E
19	A	B	C	D	E	40	A	B	C	D	E
20	A	B	C	D	E	41	A	B	C	D	E
21	A	B	C	D	E	42	A	B	C	D	E

Notes

Essential Preparation for

UMAT

UNDERGRADUATE MEDICINE & HEALTH SCIENCES ADMISSION TEST

MULTIPLE CHOICE ANSWER SHEET

Use pencil when filling out this sheet

Fill in the circle correctly				
●	(B)	(C)	(D)	(E)

If you make a mistake neatly cross it out and circle the correct response				
⊗	●	(C)	(D)	(E)

1	(A)	(B)	(C)	(D)	(E)	22	(A)	(B)	(C)	(D)	(E)
2	(A)	(B)	(C)	(D)	(E)	23	(A)	(B)	(C)	(D)	(E)
3	(A)	(B)	(C)	(D)	(E)	24	(A)	(B)	(C)	(D)	(E)
4	(A)	(B)	(C)	(D)	(E)	25	(A)	(B)	(C)	(D)	(E)
5	(A)	(B)	(C)	(D)	(E)	26	(A)	(B)	(C)	(D)	(E)
6	(A)	(B)	(C)	(D)	(E)	27	(A)	(B)	(C)	(D)	(E)
7	(A)	(B)	(C)	(D)	(E)	28	(A)	(B)	(C)	(D)	(E)
8	(A)	(B)	(C)	(D)	(E)	29	(A)	(B)	(C)	(D)	(E)
9	(A)	(B)	(C)	(D)	(E)	30	(A)	(B)	(C)	(D)	(E)
10	(A)	(B)	(C)	(D)	(E)	31	(A)	(B)	(C)	(D)	(E)
11	(A)	(B)	(C)	(D)	(E)	32	(A)	(B)	(C)	(D)	(E)
12	(A)	(B)	(C)	(D)	(E)	33	(A)	(B)	(C)	(D)	(E)
13	(A)	(B)	(C)	(D)	(E)	34	(A)	(B)	(C)	(D)	(E)
14	(A)	(B)	(C)	(D)	(E)	35	(A)	(B)	(C)	(D)	(E)
15	(A)	(B)	(C)	(D)	(E)	36	(A)	(B)	(C)	(D)	(E)
16	(A)	(B)	(C)	(D)	(E)	37	(A)	(B)	(C)	(D)	(E)
17	(A)	(B)	(C)	(D)	(E)	38	(A)	(B)	(C)	(D)	(E)
18	(A)	(B)	(C)	(D)	(E)	39	(A)	(B)	(C)	(D)	(E)
19	(A)	(B)	(C)	(D)	(E)	40	(A)	(B)	(C)	(D)	(E)
20	(A)	(B)	(C)	(D)	(E)	41	(A)	(B)	(C)	(D)	(E)
21	(A)	(B)	(C)	(D)	(E)	42	(A)	(B)	(C)	(D)	(E)

Notes

Essential Preparation for

UMAT

UNDERGRADUATE MEDICINE & HEALTH SCIENCES ADMISSION TEST

MULTIPLE CHOICE ANSWER SHEET

Use pencil when filling out this sheet

Fill in the circle correctly				
●	Ⓑ	Ⓒ	Ⓓ	Ⓔ

If you make a mistake neatly cross it out and circle the correct response				
⊗	●	Ⓒ	Ⓓ	Ⓔ

1	Ⓐ	Ⓑ	Ⓒ	Ⓓ	Ⓔ	22	Ⓐ	Ⓑ	Ⓒ	Ⓓ	Ⓔ
2	Ⓐ	Ⓑ	Ⓒ	Ⓓ	Ⓔ	23	Ⓐ	Ⓑ	Ⓒ	Ⓓ	Ⓔ
3	Ⓐ	Ⓑ	Ⓒ	Ⓓ	Ⓔ	24	Ⓐ	Ⓑ	Ⓒ	Ⓓ	Ⓔ
4	Ⓐ	Ⓑ	Ⓒ	Ⓓ	Ⓔ	25	Ⓐ	Ⓑ	Ⓒ	Ⓓ	Ⓔ
5	Ⓐ	Ⓑ	Ⓒ	Ⓓ	Ⓔ	26	Ⓐ	Ⓑ	Ⓒ	Ⓓ	Ⓔ
6	Ⓐ	Ⓑ	Ⓒ	Ⓓ	Ⓔ	27	Ⓐ	Ⓑ	Ⓒ	Ⓓ	Ⓔ
7	Ⓐ	Ⓑ	Ⓒ	Ⓓ	Ⓔ	28	Ⓐ	Ⓑ	Ⓒ	Ⓓ	Ⓔ
8	Ⓐ	Ⓑ	Ⓒ	Ⓓ	Ⓔ	29	Ⓐ	Ⓑ	Ⓒ	Ⓓ	Ⓔ
9	Ⓐ	Ⓑ	Ⓒ	Ⓓ	Ⓔ	30	Ⓐ	Ⓑ	Ⓒ	Ⓓ	Ⓔ
10	Ⓐ	Ⓑ	Ⓒ	Ⓓ	Ⓔ	31	Ⓐ	Ⓑ	Ⓒ	Ⓓ	Ⓔ
11	Ⓐ	Ⓑ	Ⓒ	Ⓓ	Ⓔ	32	Ⓐ	Ⓑ	Ⓒ	Ⓓ	Ⓔ
12	Ⓐ	Ⓑ	Ⓒ	Ⓓ	Ⓔ	33	Ⓐ	Ⓑ	Ⓒ	Ⓓ	Ⓔ
13	Ⓐ	Ⓑ	Ⓒ	Ⓓ	Ⓔ	34	Ⓐ	Ⓑ	Ⓒ	Ⓓ	Ⓔ
14	Ⓐ	Ⓑ	Ⓒ	Ⓓ	Ⓔ	35	Ⓐ	Ⓑ	Ⓒ	Ⓓ	Ⓔ
15	Ⓐ	Ⓑ	Ⓒ	Ⓓ	Ⓔ	36	Ⓐ	Ⓑ	Ⓒ	Ⓓ	Ⓔ
16	Ⓐ	Ⓑ	Ⓒ	Ⓓ	Ⓔ	37	Ⓐ	Ⓑ	Ⓒ	Ⓓ	Ⓔ
17	Ⓐ	Ⓑ	Ⓒ	Ⓓ	Ⓔ	38	Ⓐ	Ⓑ	Ⓒ	Ⓓ	Ⓔ
18	Ⓐ	Ⓑ	Ⓒ	Ⓓ	Ⓔ	39	Ⓐ	Ⓑ	Ⓒ	Ⓓ	Ⓔ
19	Ⓐ	Ⓑ	Ⓒ	Ⓓ	Ⓔ	40	Ⓐ	Ⓑ	Ⓒ	Ⓓ	Ⓔ
20	Ⓐ	Ⓑ	Ⓒ	Ⓓ	Ⓔ	41	Ⓐ	Ⓑ	Ⓒ	Ⓓ	Ⓔ
21	Ⓐ	Ⓑ	Ⓒ	Ⓓ	Ⓔ	42	Ⓐ	Ⓑ	Ⓒ	Ⓓ	Ⓔ